Pauline Golya

THE OLD TORQUAY POTTERIES

Plate I. An interval of about fifty years separates these two articles made at the Watcombe Pottery. The classical-style vase of the eighteen-seventies typifies the early terracotta wares, while the 'Cottage' plate represents a type of slip decoration practiced by most of the Torquay potteries in the first quarter of the present century.

THE
OLD TORQUAY POTTERIES

From Castle to Cottage

by

D. & E. LLOYD THOMAS

ARTHUR H. STOCKWELL LTD.,
Elms Court, Ilfracombe, Devon.
In association with
GUILDART – LONDON

Also by E. Lloyd Thomas:
Victorian Art Pottery

ISBN 0 7223 1103-6
Printed in Great Britain by
Arthur H. Stockwell Ltd
Elms Court   Ilfracombe
Devon

When the dust of the workshop is still,
the dust of the workman at rest,
May some generous heart find a will
to seek and to cherish his best.

Eden Phillpotts

Preface

In comparison with factories in other parts of the country the potteries of the Torquay district of South Devon have received little serious attention from critics, historians, or collectors since the end of the nineteenth century. This may be because the description 'Torquay pottery' often brings to mind no more than a red earthenware cup or teapot decorated with a thatched cottage and bearing an inscription such as: 'Du ee 'ave a cup o' tay'. But there was a great deal to Torquay pottery besides the popular Motto Ware. In fact, the story of the industry, from its initial successes in the 1870s with high quality terracotta to its final rôle as a supplier of holiday souvenirs, forms a fascinating, if relatively brief, episode in the history of English ceramics. It is also a story that deserves to be recorded before it is completely forgotten.

In our *Victorian Art Pottery* we devoted a section to the wares, mainly of unglazed terracotta in classical forms, produced by the early Torquay firms during the last thirty years of the nineteenth century. In the present book we have not only given a fuller description of this first period, but have extended the account to include the potteries and wares of the twentieth century up to the final closure of the Watcombe factory in 1962. We have not attempted to compile a catalogue of all known types of Torquay pottery; this would be virtually impossible. We have, instead, tried to describe the main kinds of ware and styles of decoration produced by the various firms, so that readers may be able to recognize and date examples they encounter.

All the potteries described have now been demolished or adapted to other purposes, and their records appear to have been destroyed. In these circumstances the most reliable evidence of their activities consists of the wares themselves, supplemented with what little is available from contemporary magazines and trade publications. Over a period of many years we have paid frequent visits to the sites of all the old Works in order to obtain first-hand impressions, and have examined many thousands of articles of Torquay pottery in private and public collections. We have also been fortunate in meeting a number of persons who either worked in the potteries or were closely associated with them. Their accounts of day-to-day business in the various firms, and their recollections of the people involved, have been invaluable in creating an impression of the Torquay potteries as a living industry rather than a collection of dry facts and artefacts.

It is, perhaps, inevitable when breaking new ground that some of the information collected should prove to be contradictory or ambiguous. Wherever possible we have checked our 'facts' from alternative sources, but when this has not been possible we have presented them with appropriate caution. New material is continually coming to light, mainly through the efforts of members of the recently-formed Torquay Pottery Collectors' Society, and this book should be regarded only as a first attempt to present an integrated account of the subject.

Although Torquay pottery is, as yet, seldom seen in the larger sale-rooms, it has an intrinsic character that is lacking in many other contemporary wares, such as the Staffordshire 'flat-backs' and continental 'fairings' that have become so popular in recent years. The chief reason for this is that the factories concerned represented one of the last centres of the pottery industry to operate by traditional methods using local materials. Even though batch production was normal practice, the wares still retained an individuality that identified them with the spirit of the Arts and Crafts movement at least as closely as those of many, more fashionable, Art potteries. As a result, Torquay ware of all kinds offers a relatively new and interesting field, both to the enterprising collector and to the student of English ceramics. It has the further advantages of being widely distributed and still, except for the early terracotta, comparatively inexpensive.

Acknowledgements

In preparing this book we have been grateful for the assistance afforded by the many individuals and organizations who have allowed us to inspect and photograph articles of pottery, and to consult material in their possession, or have supplied us with other information on the Torquay potteries.

In particular, we wish to thank the following:
Mr Harry Birbeck; Mr K. Bond, formerly of the Devon Tors Pottery; Mr W. Gordon Brewer; Mr N.D. Caldwell; Mr and Mrs H.T. Carden; Mr Arthur Cole, formerly of the Watcombe and Longpark potteries, and Mrs Cole; Mr Ian M. Green; Mr I.G. Hardy, Exeter Central Library; Dr N. Harris, Curator, Torquay Natural History Society's Museum; Mr R.J. Head, formerly of the Torquay Pottery; Mr and Mrs W.G. Hester; Mr Simon Hunt, Curator of Applied Art, Royal Albert Memorial Museum, Exeter; Mrs V. Jenkins; Mr J. Knight; Mr L. Manley, formerly of the Bovey Pottery; Mrs L. Meakin; Mrs Overill, of the Domestic Trading Co., Newton Abbot; Mr J.R. Pike, Torquay Central Library; Mr S. Reed; Mrs S. Vallance.

Unfortunately certain others who, as the local saying goes, 'had it in mind to write', have never done so. In these circumstances we can do no more than echo the sentiments with which Llewellynn Jewitt concluded the Introduction to his *Ceramic Art of Great Britain*, and regret that this book is not as complete as it might have been.

Contents

Note: *The marks used by the various Potteries will be found at the end of the corresponding Section of the text. They are not necessarily drawn to scale.*

List of Line Drawings

List of Colour Plates

List of Monochrome Plates

B

SECTION THREE: HELE CROSS

3.1 The Torquay Terra-Cotta Company

SECTION FIVE: LONGPARK

SECTION SIX: THE SMALLER POTTERIES

SECTION SEVEN: OTHER TORQUAY-TYPE POTTERIES

Section One

INTRODUCTION

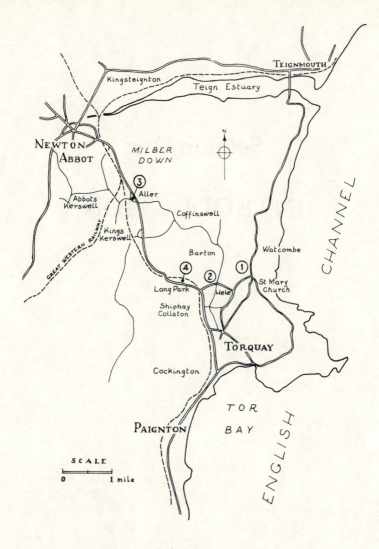

Fig. i. Sketch map of the region between Torquay and Newton Abbot, showing the sites of the larger potteries.

1. Watcombe Terra-Cotta Works/Pottery, St. Marychurch.
2. Torquay Terra-Cotta Works/Pottery, Hele Cross.
3. Aller (Vale) Pottery.
4. Longpark Terra-Cotta Works/Pottery.

O thou sculptor, painter, poet!
Take this lesson to thy heart:
That is best which lieth nearest:
Shape from that thy work of art.

Longfellow: Gaspar Becerra.

Little more than a century has elapsed since ornamental earthenware was first made in the Torquay district of South Devon from the local red clay. Yet what was hailed in the nineteenth century as a new and important 'Art Industry', and one which eventually involved over a dozen potteries, is now virtually extinct. This industry owed its existence to the chance discovery of a bed of fine red terracotta clay in the grounds of Watcombe House, just north of Torquay itself. But nothing might have come of the discovery if it had not been for a combination of economic and social circumstances that is unlikely ever to occur again. It is appropriate, therefore, to begin by recalling something of the status of the English pottery industry in the middle of Queen Victoria's reign and of the fashionable trends in the domestic arts of the period.

Until the latter part of the eighteenth century the manufacture of pottery in this country had been widely distributed. Wherever beds of clay could be found near to supplies of fuel for burning it into earthenware there was usually a Pottery serving local needs. Although some of these

25

potteries became sufficiently well established over the years to be regarded as permanent industries — as at Rye in Sussex and Barnstaple in North Devon — the development of the coal mines in the Midlands and North Country, where coal seams often alternated with beds of clay, gradually led to the concentration of pottery manufacture in these districts. In this way 'The Potteries' of Staffordshire had become the main source of domestic earthenware by the second quarter of the nineteenth century, not only for the British Isles but also for the Continent and the Americas.

Originally, Staffordshire pottery had been made from local clays of whatever colour happened to be available. In the course of time, however, improved means of transport enabled white clay to be brought from the West of England in response to the demand for pottery that had the desirable whiteness of foreign porcelain. One of the sources of this white clay was, and still is, the Teign valley in South Devon, not far from Torquay. Yet, owing to the lack of coal, only a few small potteries existed in the district during the first half of the nineteenth century.

The early Victorian Staffordshire wares were intended mainly for working- and middle-class families, and certainly provided good value for money. A few manufacturers, like Minton and Wedgwood, catered for the better-quality market with various kinds of fine earthenwares but, generally speaking, pottery was regarded as the poor man's china. Those who could afford porcelain — the wealthy aristocracy and the *nouveau riche* manufacturers — still chose it, or its English counterpart bone china, both for table-wares and for ornamental vases and figures.

This tendency to look down on pottery persisted at least until the late 1850s, by which time the good taste of the eighteenth century had been swamped by the flood of badly-designed domestic furnishings produced in the factories of the new industrial towns. The customers for these articles demanded that they should 'look the money', and good design soon became confused with ostentation, excessive ornament-ation, and sheer fussiness. Because it was not so fashionable, pottery did not suffer quite as much as china from the decorative excesses of the mid-Victorian period. Nevertheless, the factory-made wares lost much of the character previously associated with hand-thrown pottery, and acquired a machine-made uniformity that was in keeping with most other industrial products.

The Arts and Crafts Movement

There was, inevitably, a reaction to the over-decoration of domestic articles by those artists and critics who still retained a basic understanding of good design and were anxious to re-educate people in matters of taste. One of the first moves in this direction was taken by the Royal Society of Arts which, in 1846, held a competition for designs suitable for 'Art Manufactures'. This was a deliberate attempt to create an interest in household goods that were of inherently good artistic design and yet capable of being produced by factory methods.

Another, and more lasting, stimulus to the appreciation of art by the middle classes was given by the legalization (also in 1846) of the lotteries conducted by the Art Union of London. The original object of this organization and, later, of Art Unions in other parts of the country, was the distribution as prizes of original works of art from the Royal Academy exhibitions and elsewhere. In the course of time, however, the Art Unions themselves began to commission limited editions of articles, including decorative pottery, for distribution as smaller prizes to their members. This practice continued throughout the nineteenth century and enabled many people to acquire minor works of art that they would otherwise have been unable to afford.

Even so, the years just before and after the Great Exhibition of 1851, described by one cynic as: 'that monument to bad taste', were not the best time to foster a wider understanding of good design by the general public. In fact, another decade was to elapse before the first practical and effective steps in support of a return to a simpler style of domestic furnishing, based on the idea of 'honest craftsmanship', were taken by William Morris. Morris, who started with an amateur's interest in the arts and a horror of the factory system and all its works, eventually set up his own business to produce individually designed and mostly hand-made furnishings. Although some of Morris's decorative schemes now seem fussy and overpowering they were comparatively restrained by mid-Victorian standards. The products of his firm included stained glass, metalwork, and furniture; but he is now remembered chiefly for his wallpaper and textile designs, some of which are still being printed.

Morris inevitably lost his battle against the factory system because he could not compete in price with mass-produced goods, but he converted many people to his way of thinking and created a limited demand for individually-made domestic articles of good appearance and sound design. This fashion was reflected by the formation of several other associations of artist-craftsmen during the 1880s with aims similar to those of Morris's own firm. Amongst these was the Arts and Crafts Exhibition Society, founded in 1888 by a group of prominent designers, whose purpose Morris was to summarize by saying:

'Our art is the work of a small minority composed of educated persons, fully conscious of their aim of producing beauty, and distinguished from the great body of workmen by the possession of that aim.'

Morris's practical experience of ceramics was limited to tile painting, but this did not prevent him from laying down certain rules which he considered should be observed in the making of artistic pottery. These were:

(i)   Articles should not be moulded if they can be made on the wheel, or in some other way by hand.

(ii) Pottery should not be finished by turning in a lathe.

(iii) Excessive neatness is undesirable, especially in cheap wares.

(iv) Pottery should not be decorated by printing, and painted decoration should be confined to what can only be done on pottery.

Art Pottery

At a time of intense commercial competition Morris's precepts were ignored by most of the established pottery and china manufacturers. Nevertheless, his appeal for a revival of craftsmanship, supported by the writings of John Ruskin, met with the approval of the younger and *avant-garde* section of the public. It also resulted in a widespread movement for the establishment of Arts and Crafts Schools in various parts of the country to train students who could not attend the existing institutions in Central London. One of the first of these was the Lambeth School of Art in South London. Lambeth had been a centre of pottery manufacture for over 200 years, and it was only natural that pottery decoration and modelling should have been amongst the subjects taught. During the 'sixties the Lambeth firm of Doulton & Co., which specialized in saltglazed stoneware and terracotta (mostly of a utilitarian kind), had collaborated with students of the Art School in the making and firing of individually decorated articles of pottery. As a result, Doulton's were persuaded in 1871 to set up a special department for the production of what had by then become known as 'Art' pottery. This represented a deliberate attempt to break away from the mechanical perfection of the white china of the Potteries and to create works of art in earthenware and stoneware. Doulton's 'Lambeth Art Studios', as they were called, were staffed mainly with ex-students of Lambeth School of Art and their efforts were well received, both by the critics and by the public.

The success of the wares made by Doulton's and other studio-type potteries, such as those of the Martin brothers and William De Morgan, led to a fashion for Art pottery to go with other furnishings made in the same spirit. That it was pottery, rather than porcelain, which received this approval was characteristic of the Arts and Crafts movement, which regarded the former as a native tradition — in contrast to the foreign, and therefore unworthy, origin of the latter.

The revival of decorative pottery, and especially pottery made from dark-coloured clays in imitation of early country wares, stimulated a renewed interest in terracotta. In Victorian times the word 'terracotta' could mean almost any unglazed earthenware, usually with a red or brown body but occasionally pale buff or cream, when it was called 'white terracotta'. Red earthenware had, of course, been in common use in Mediterranean countries since early times, but it had never been popular in Britain for ornamental wares, except as flower pots and garden urns. By the middle of the nineteenth century, though, a few firms in Staffordshire and elsewhere were already making vases, plaques, and architectural features in terracotta, and the Jury of the 1851 Exhibition had urged manufacturers to take a greater interest in this material.

Watcombe Clay

Even the most casual visitor to South Devon can hardly fail to notice the dark colour of the soil, and as far back as the sixteenth century licences had been granted for the excavation of 'red earth'. But the potters of the eighteenth and early nineteenth centuries were always searching for ever whiter materials to emulate porcelain, and the dark clays of the Torquay region had been ignored.

It was in these circumstances that red clay was rediscovered in the grounds of Watcombe House in 1869. The owner, a Mr G.J. Allen, was a cultivated man and quick to realize the potential value of the clay to sculptors and potters. After tests had confirmed that it was ideally suited to the manufacture of terracotta, Mr Allen formed a company to raise the material and sell it to potteries in other parts of the country. However, when the unique qualities of the clay became apparent, it was decided (according to Llewellynn Jewitt, the contemporary ceramic historian) 'to erect a pottery on the spot and to convert the clay immediately from the pits into Art-manufactures and architectural enrichments.'

The Watcombe Pottery, as it eventually became known, was established at just the right moment to take advantage of the fashion for Art pottery, which reached its peak during the thirty years from 1870 to 1900. At the beginning of the nineteenth century Torquay had been only a small fishing village, but during the Napoleonic wars the British fleet often used Tor Bay as an anchorage and the first residential villas erected on the wooded slopes above the harbour were built for naval officers. The place soon acquired a reputation for its mild climate and attractive setting and, with the arrival of the railway in the middle of the century, it became a popular resort of 'invalids and persons of delicate constitution'. From

Plate II.   Terracotta portrait plaque of Charles Brock, the first Manager and Art Director of the Watcombe Terra-Cotta Clay Co., by J.M. Mohr. Inscribed: 'J.M. Mohr, 1873. C. Brock, Watcombe'.

the point of view of a prospective pottery manufacturer the railway provided two important services. It enabled coal to be transported easily and cheaply from the Midlands and South Wales to fire the kilns, and it brought in holiday and residential visitors who were all potential customers for fashionable pottery.

In these circumstances the Watcombe Pottery found a ready market for its products, which were highly praised in the art magazines of the time and displayed at numerous national and international exhibitions. But the success of the firm was virtually guaranteed when, in 1873, Queen Victoria 'graciously consented to accept' a pair of Watcombe water bottles as a birthday present from Baroness Burdett-Coutts, who was then living in Torquay. Since the baroness was regarded as the wealthiest woman in the country she (and the Queen) must have thought very highly of the articles to choose them in preference to a gift of greater intrinsic value.

The initial success of the enterprise soon led to the discovery of other beds of the red clay in the district just north of Torquay and in 1875 another firm, calling itself the 'Torquay Terra-Cotta Company', was established at Hele Cross to make similar wares. In 1881 an existing Pottery near Kings Kerswell, between Torquay and Newton Abbot, later known as the Aller Vale Pottery, also went over to the production of terracotta and other Art wares after having previously been concerned with the manufacture of simple domestic articles and builders' goods.

'Modern Terra-cotta-ry'

All three of the early Torquay potteries originally set out to produce terracotta wares which relied for their appeal mainly on their shape and natural colour, sometimes with a little formal decoration such as enamelled motifs or gilt borders. The general style first adopted at Watcombe and Hele Cross was predominantly classical, with vases and figures derived from Graeco-Roman originals, although copies of works by contemporary sculptors were also popular. Despite the fact that most of the wares were formed by moulding or casting, and the vases finished by turning, they were accepted as a valid type of Art pottery and during the 'seventies and early 'eighties both firms were very successful in promoting terracotta as a fashionable decorative material. So much so that W.S. Gilbert, in the Savoy opera *Patience* (first produced in 1881), poked fun at the vogue with references to the ideal husband as one who was:

'such a judge of blue-and-white and other kinds of pottery — from early Oriental to modern terra-cotta-ry.'

It must be remembered, though, that the average domestic furnishing style of this period was almost as fussy as in the 1850s, and many of the classically inspired Watcombe vases must have seemed even more austere at the time they were made than they do to present-day collectors. In fact, the early Torquay pottery would have been more at home in the late Georgian and Regency period some seventy years earlier. In consequence, after the initial enthusiasm for the ware, the novelty of plain terracotta began to pall, and the average customer began to expect a greater variety of treatment and decoration.

Apart from Gothic, which was already outmoded and never affected the Torquay potteries, there were plenty of other styles to choose from. Gilbert was nothing if not topical, and his mention of Oriental and 'blue-and-white' pottery in *Patience* was a reference to the contemporary fashion for Chinese and Japanese ceramics and imitations of them. Another influence in the 'eighties was the Aesthetic movement, which had developed out of the Arts and Crafts movement. The Aesthetes favoured simplicity of form and naturalism in ornament, based on their own definitions of beauty, and were addicted to certain decorative emblems such as the lily and the sunflower. And, as if these new sources of inspiration did not offer enough scope, some manufacturers went even further in their search for novelty by copying the pottery styles of ancient American and near-Eastern civilizations.

The Transition to Glazed Pottery

Against this confused background the situation of the Torquay terracotta factories in the mid-'eighties was summed up rather dogmatically by J.F. Blacker who, referring to

Watcombe in his *19th Century English Ceramic Art*, wrote:

'. . . . art-school inspiration, classical figures and busts, with those of modern men, were not likely to lead to success, therefore the scope of the work was extended to include decorative pottery.'

Blacker did not explain what he meant by 'decorative', but one result of this change of policy was the introduction of figures in contemporary dress and sentimental attitudes, as alternatives to the earlier classical models. Another was the general adoption of oil painting as a cheap method of providing large areas of brightly coloured decoration on vases and plaques. At the same time the earlier practice of enamelling narrow borders and repeated motifs was extended to include the decoration of ornamental wares with birds, flowers and fish; done in a natural style direct on to the unglazed terracotta. A small amount of very high quality ware was also produced, both at Watcombe and by the Torquay Terra-Cotta Company, using conventional underglaze decorating techniques, often on a prepared white ground. This last type of work could, of course, hardly be described as terracotta, even though it still had a red body underneath, and it was then only a small step to the general introduction of glazed wares.

It was the Aller Vale Pottery, however, that succeeded in combining the forms and styles of decoration of earlier civilizations with traditional West Country techniques to produce a new type of Art ware that eventually replaced terracotta as the standard product of the Torquay factories in the twentieth century.

The Aller wares had never been as sophisticated as those of the Watcombe and Hele Cross factories, and by 1890 this firm was already beginning to cater for a new class of customer — the holiday visitor. In earlier days visitors had come to Torquay for a season, perhaps for the whole winter. They had leisure, they wished to be in the fashion, and they followed (some of them, at least) the current trends in art. More important, they were willing to spend money in acquiring examples of the latest style of pottery. But towards the end of the century the residential visitor was being replaced by the holidaymaker. Later still, with the development of the motor car, came the tourist. These customers were not necessarily interested in Art pottery or classical vases. They merely wanted

c

something bright and cheap to take home as a souvenir, with the result that the local potteries had, again, either to adapt their products to meet the new demand or go out of business.

The usual type of decoration employed at Aller Vale consisted of designs painted in thick coloured slips on articles that had been prepared with a dip coat of slip of a uniform colour and were subsequently finished with a rich, clear, glaze. Such treatment was often associated with little rhymes or proverbs scratched through the ground, so that the lettering showed up in the dark red colour of the body. This 'Motto Ware' became very popular with visitors in the early part of the present century, and is what most people now think of as 'Torquay pottery'. Indeed, so successful was the Aller Vale Pottery in meeting the contemporary demand for 'quaintness', as it was called, that its wares were sold by Liberty's, the London store famous for its Art furnishings. This brought the firm to the notice of the fashionable world and also secured for it the patronage of members of the Royal Family.

By the end of Queen Victoria's reign the hey-day of the Arts and Crafts movement was almost over, and the Watcombe and Torquay Terra-Cotta Companies were finding it difficult to keep going with what had come to be regarded as their traditional terracotta wares. The high fashion was now for Art Nouveau, with its tall, sinuous, decorative motifs; but this short-lived style made little impression on the South Devon potteries and, after experimenting with glazed wares for a few years, the Torquay Terra-Cotta Company went out of business about 1905. The Watcombe Pottery, however, secured a new lease of life in 1901, when it was combined with Aller Vale to form the 'Royal Aller Vale and Watcombe Art Potteries'. Despite the name, Watcombe was evidently the dominant member of the combine, and the Aller Works were run down and eventually closed soon after the Great War. By this time Watcombe had gone over to the manufacture of Aller-type wares and introduced many new patterns of its own. In this way the firm was able to continue for a further forty years until it, too, was obliged to close in 1962.

The Later Firms

During the first quarter of the present century a further change took place in the Torquay pottery industry. Whereas in the nineteenth century it had been dominated by the Watcombe and Hele Cross firms, the increasing demand for holiday souvenirs now led to the establishment of several new, and mostly smaller, potteries on the northern outskirts of the town. The largest of these was the Longpark Pottery on the Newton Road, although this business had originally been started as a terrcotta works in the late 'eighties. Others included a new Torquay Pottery on the old Terra-Cotta Company's premises, the Barton and Daison Potteries, and one or two minor firms in the St. Marychurch district. Indeed, from the number of articles to be found that bear factory marks of the time, the years just before and just after the Great War must have been the most productive period of the industry.

Most of these later firms were founded and run by men who had previously worked at one or other of the older potteries and it is not surprising, therefore, that in their early days they tended to copy the styles of pottery evolved by Aller Vale and Watcombe. They even used the same decoration codes, as if they were the common property of the industry!

Most of the twentieth-century firms eventually introduced distinctive patterns of their own, such as Longpark's Cockerels and the Torquay Pottery's Parrot vases. But by the beginning of the Great War slip decoration was going out of fashion, except for the traditional designs, and the patterns introduced after about 1915 were generally done in pigment colours, although still on an overall slip ground. Unfortunately, the Torquay potteries were always copying one another, and it is often impossible to decide where a certain style of decoration really originated. This is particularly true of the popular Kingfisher design which, although claimed by Watcombe, is mostly found on Longpark wares, and was imitated as far afield as the Western-super-Mare Pottery in North Somerset. Yet other patterns seem to have been the speciality of individual decorators, who painted them on the wares of whichever firm they happened to be working for at the time.

Unfortunately, the Torquay potteries never publicized the names of their decorators, or even encouraged them to sign their work. As a result, fully signed articles are rare, and our knowledge of the decorators themselves is derived mainly from other sources.

This habit of moving from one firm to another was probably a tradition brought by the original decorators at the Watcombe and Torquay Terra-Cotta Works from the Staffordshire Potteries, where it was the accepted way of gaining experience and bettering one's position. But for locally engaged employees who wished to improve their knowledge of design and decoration there was the Vivian Institute in Torquay itself. This had been established in 1878 to provide instruction in Art and Science and was attended by students from as far away as Bovey Tracey. In its own way the Vivian Institute must have been as important for the development and exchange of ideas in the Torquay pottery industry as the Lambeth School of Art had been to Doulton's Pottery in London. Yet many of the artists who had trained there were obliged to alternate their decorating work with spells of employment of an entirely different kind when business was slack at the potteries. Other decorators, particularly the older and more accomplished, solved the same problem by taking pupils themselves, or by doing studio painting in their spare time.

The depression of the 'thirties, followed by the Second World War, took its toll of the Torquay potteries, and after the War only Watcombe, Longpark, and a few small firms continued making decorated red earthenware. By the middle of the century, even the small amount of hand work involved was becoming uneconomic, and Longpark finally shut down in 1957. The closure of Watcombe five years later marked the virtual end of the red clay pottery industry in Torquay, and the one or two firms still working in the district appear to have gone over mainly to the production of white slip-cast wares with no particular local characteristics.

When the Torquay terracotta industry was established in the 1870s the products of the Watcombe and Hele Cross factories were acclaimed by connoisseurs as a new form of Art ware — to be displayed at International Exhibitions and praised in the art magazines. But by the end of the Great War the initial wave of enthusiasm was over and the industry had been reduced to being mainly a source of holiday souvenirs. This change of emphasis from 'art for art's sake' to a purely commercial attitude may be illustrated with two contrasting quotations. The first is taken from the *Art-Journal* which, in 1872, wrote of the Watcombe Pottery:

'It is worthy of note, also, that the directors are not mere speculators, who would sacrifice any amount of reputation to gain, ... for such prosperity enables them to issue works of great beauty — works that do not immediately find purchasers.'

The second, briefer and in keeping with the times, is the reply said to have been made by the proprietor of a Torquay pottery in the nineteen-thirties to an old workman who complained of the pouring qualities of the firm's teapots:

"They aren't made to pour, lad — they're made to sell."

'Those Grand Old Artists'

Because of this change in attitude very little serious attention has been paid to the later Torquay wares, and even contemporary guide books dismiss the local potteries in a few words. Perhaps the best account of the industry at the beginning of the present century is that given in Eden Phillpotts' novel *Brunel's Tower*, published in 1915. Although written as fiction, this story of day-to-day life in a Torquay pottery is clearly based on the old pumping-house of Brunel's atmospheric railway which was occupied by the Longpark Pottery. Since Eden Phillpotts was a South Devon man, and obviously familiar with the processes involved in the local potteries, the book is as good a description of the manufacture of Torquay pottery as could be wished for. Even the various styles of decoration are described in detail and the book should be read by every serious collector of Torquay ware. Unfortunately, it is difficult to tell whether the story consistently describes the working of this one Pottery or whether, as seems more likely, it is an amalgam of Phillpotts' knowledge of the industry as a whole.

Despite the fact that these later wares have been neglected in comparison with the earlier unglazed terracotta, they have a character which identifies them as 'Torquay' as unmistakeably as the pink splash-lustred jugs of an earlier period are recognized as 'Sunderland'. And, just as Sunderland lustre ware is now highly prized and collected for its transfer-printed verses, so are the Torquay slip-wares coming to be collected for their colourful decoration and scratched mottoes.

Although the Torquay pottery industry differed from its Staffordshire counterpart in that it was mainly concerned with the manufacture of decorative, rather than utilitarian, wares it would be rash to assert that any firm did *not* make a particular type of ware or style of decoration. The most that can be said is that certain articles, such as toilet sets, dinner services, and wall tiles are rarely found; probably because they were hardly the kind of thing to be bought by visitors as a memento of a holiday in Devon. Watcombe produced most things in its time, from terracotta angels to advertisements for soap. At the turn of the century it was even making grotesque cats and dogs. This would have amused Jerome K. Jerome who, in 1888, had prophesied to the readers of *Three Men in a Boat* that the spotted 'china' dogs of the Victorian mantlepiece would be dug up two hundred years later by archaeologists and admired for their delicate beauty. As he put it: "We shall be referred to lovingly as 'those grand old artists that flourished in the nineteenth century, and produced those china dogs'." We may wonder, therefore, whether 'J' would have been surprised that, in less than half the time he predicted, such things might be happening with all kinds of Torquay pottery. Possibly not, for it was just those Victorians who despised spotted dogs who admired the artistic 'quaintness' of Aller Vale jugs and vases. And who would now gainsay Jerome's further prediction that: "travellers from Japan will buy up all the 'Presents from Ramsgate' and 'Souvenirs of Margate' that may have escaped destruction, and take them back to Jedo as ancient English curios"? *Autre temps, autre moeurs . . . !*

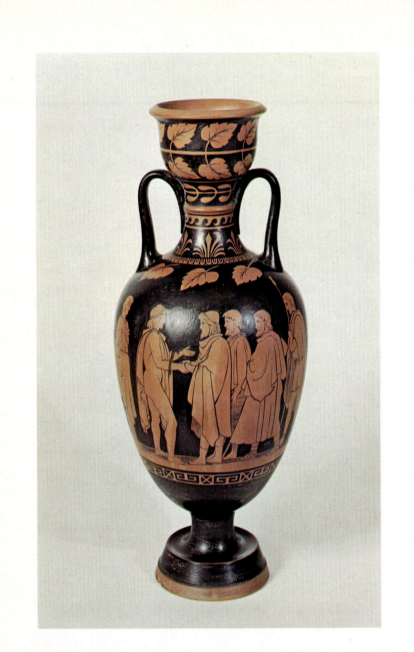

Plate III. One of a pair of large Watcombe terracotta vases, decorated in
black oil paint with classical subjects in the style of Etruscan 'red figure' ware.
Height: 530 mm (21 in). Marks: No. 2, with '336' impressed. c. 1873.

Section Two

WATCOMBE

2.1. THE WATCOMBE TERRA-COTTA CLAY COMPANY

Vases and urns and bas-reliefs,
Memorials of forgotten griefs,
Or records of heroic deeds
Of demi-gods and mighty chiefs . . .

Longfellow: *Keramos.*

Until the middle of the nineteenth century St. Mary Church (written as three words) was a village quite separate from Torquay; a cluster of houses, dominated by the square tower of the church itself, on the high ground between the Teignmouth Road and the sea. Yet even then the Victorian builders were filling the intervening one-and-a-half miles with stuccoed villas, and St. Marychurch is now just a northern suburb of the modern Borough of Torbay.

Beyond St. Marychurch the countryside is still dotted with substantial Victorian houses in their well-wooded estates; built by wealthy gentlemen as retirement homes following the construction of the South Devon Railway in the second quarter of the century. The great Isambard Brunel, who was Engineer to the railway company, planned a home for himself in the district, but died before it was completed. Another of these country houses, originally known as Watcombe House, is situated about half a mile north of St. Marychurch at the head of a picturesque valley running down to the sea, with the red cliffs of Watcombe towering behind.

In the late eighteen-sixties Watcombe House was occupied

41

by a Mr G.J. Allen, son of a Bishop of Ely and retired Master (i.e. headmaster) of Dulwich College. Various stories are told of the circumstances surrounding the discovery of red pottery clay in the grounds of the house. One version has it that Mr Allen's attention was drawn by his butler to the character of the clay dug up when a well was being sunk. Another is that given in the *Art-Journal* of 1878 by Professor T.C. Archer, who wrote:

'. . . . whilst the labourers were digging out the trenches for the foundations, he (Mr Allen) was much struck with the peculiarly unctuous nature of the clay they threw out; and under the impression that it was of an unusual character, he took samples to the potteries of Bovey Tracey, Worcester, and Staffordshire, and obtained opinions after experiments with them, which convinced him that the clay was a valuable and, in this country, unique, pottery clay.'

A New Industry

When it was realized that the Watcombe clay was ideally suited to the manufacture of terracotta, and far superior to anything else then available in other parts of the country, Mr Allen decided to establish a business to exploit the discovery. In 1869* he therefore formed a Limited Company of 'seven gentlemen', with himself as Chairman, called 'The Watcombe Terra-Cotta Clay Company' to raise the clay and offer it for sale to existing potteries. Strange as it may now seem, this venture was undertaken with the ostensible object of providing employment in the district, rather than profit for the directors, the *Art-Journal* commenting:

'It is worthy of note, also, that the directors are not mere speculators, who would sacrifice any amount of reputation to gain. (They) are gentlemen very intimate with Art; and, in some instances, closely connected with it.'

*This is the date given by Llewellynn Jewitt, who was usually well-informed, in his *Ceramic Art of Great Britain*. In its advertisements and letter-headings the firm claimed that it was founded in 1867, but this may have been the year when the clay was first discovered.

The clay was originally dug from a small field between Watcombe House and the Teignmouth Road, at a spot now used as a car park. At first, operations were under the supervision of a Mr William Lomax, who was described as Clerk of Works, and it would be interesting to know who were the early customers. Perhaps the new company found it difficult to sell the clay, because it was not long before the proprietors decided to erect a pottery to make terracotta locally. Since there was no expertise available in the neighbourhood a Mr Charles Brock, said to have been a master potter from Hanley in Staffordshire, was persuaded to join the firm as Manager and Art Director.

It is not known for certain where Mr Brock worked before he came to Watcombe. One obvious possibility is that he had some previous experience of terracotta, which has always been regarded as a very specialized branch of the potter's art. Another and more probable theory, in view of his apparent familiarity with classical styles, is that he came from a firm such as Wedgwood's that specialized in jasper-ware with classical-type applied decoration.

Mr Brock's first task was to plan the Works and supervise their construction. The site chosen was an area of level ground by the side of the Teignmouth Road, just north of St. Marychurch village and about half a mile from Watcombe House, and the buildings were erected between 1870 and 1871. Experts in the various processes of terracotta manufacture, including mould-making, modelling, and turning, were recruited from Staffordshire, while unskilled labour was engaged locally, and in a remarkably short time the Works began to produce a wide range of high-quality wares. The team of skilled craftsmen included a Mr Henry Brewer (modeller), together with a Mr Foster and a Mr Shenton; the fact that Mr Brewer is known to have worked for Wedgwood's before coming to Watcombe lending support to the theory that Mr Brock himself had previously been associated with that famous Staffordshire firm. Another modeller was a Mr J.G. Skinner.

The original intention was to reproduce well-known examples of sculpture and pottery from antiquity, and to re-establish a fashion for classical and renaissance forms.

During this first period, which lasted until the late 'seventies, moulds were made for a very large number of objects, ranging from figure groups and busts to 'architectural enrichments' and domestic ornaments. It is doubtful whether any of these articles were made by throwing on the potter's wheel, even symmetrical vases being produced by slip-casting and finished by turning in the lathe. In this way a smooth semi-matt surface was obtained which had sufficient 'finish' to be fired without any glaze.

Classical Terracotta

The decorative treatments applied to most of the early wares were comparatively restrained; the intention being to emphasize the form and colour of the articles produced. The original Watcombe clay had a remarkably fine texture, and fired to a medium red colour, although the final shade depended to some extent on the temperature in the kiln. Some of the earliest pieces were left quite undecorated, but it is more usual to find vases ornamented with swags of flowers or other motifs that were moulded separately and applied before firing. This applied decoration was often of great delicacy, and was generally done either in a paler clay or in a white clay that had been stained light blue.

Alternatively, or in addition, selected areas of an article might be treated with blue or matt black slip; or with a turquoise blue enamel, described as 'celeste', which contrasted very well with the colour of the terracotta. This enamel was often applied in bands round the feet or necks of vases, or to decorative features such as medallions, and was sometimes associated with borders of black, transfer-printed, designs (Fig.1). It was also used to protect areas subject to handling, or to render the terracotta impervious to liquids, as on the insides of teacups. Some articles had lines of gilding applied to rims, foot-rings, or other details, but this finishing touch has often been worn away by constant handling. Other enamel colours used at this time for lining and details included dark blue, stone, and puce.

In contrast, some of the larger and more important pieces

were sometimes painted all over with classical figures and borders in imitation of 'Etruscan'* red-figure ware. Plate III, for example, shows a two-handled vase of this kind which has the figures left in the natural surface against a semi-matt black ground. Yet another decorative device was to apply a thin wash of light-coloured slip round the body of a vase to serve as a background to the decoration (Fig.2). This slip wash was made by reducing the red clay with white clay obtained from Bovey Heathfield, a few miles inland. Another vase of this type, decorated with a frieze of classical figures, outlined by black transfer-printing and coloured-in by hand, is shown in Fig. 3. The same technique was used to emphasize the drapery on statuettes. Alternatively the tones could be reversed, with the figure in a light colour and the drapery dark; while on some more elaborate compositions three shades of terracotta are present.

It is not clear why it was decided to adopt a predominantly classical style at a time when this kind of decoration was beginning to go out of fashion. As a classical scholar Mr Allen may have been unfamiliar with contemporary art trends, or it may have been simply that many of the original antique vases and sculptures were made of terracotta and the Pottery was intent on copying them in the same material. Nevertheless, the early Watcombe products were made to high technical and artistic standards and were well received by many connoisseurs.

The firm staged a display of its wares at the International Exhibition of 1872 in London, and the August issue of the *Art-Journal* of that year devoted considerable space to what it described as: 'one of the happiest issues of speculative venture that has ever been arrived at in so short a time.' Already the Pottery was employing some 80 persons: 'many of them women and girls working under the direction of skilled hands from Staffordshire.' The *Art-Journal* account then lists the types of articles made in Watcombe terracotta, saying:

'It has been fashioned into elegant vases, endless in their variety of shape and ornamentation, mantlepiece spill vases, statues and statuettes, jars, water bottles, match boxes,

*This kind of pottery is now known to have been made in Greece in the 5th century B.C.

tazzas, garden vases, ornamented flower borders for conservatories, groups for terraces, halls and entrances, baskets of flowers, etc.'

A similar display was also mounted at the Philadelphia Exhibition of 1876, and Fig. 4 shows a group of some of the further types of articles included on that occasion. Incidentally, some of the early Watcombe statues and vases were of massive proportions, being intended for decorating the halls and conservatories of large Victorian houses, although most of the domestic articles were necessarily of more modest size.

Figures and Busts

Besides hollow-wares of classical, renaissance, and even Egyptian derivation, Watcombe produced busts and statuettes of contemporary and historical celebrities, including Dickens, Scott, and Shakespeare. The 'baskets of flowers' mentioned by the *Art-Journal* were entirely hand-modelled by a Samuel Kirkland, and were reputed to have been of extreme delicacy and indicative of the plasticity and fine texture of the Watcombe clay: 'the results far surpassing anything, either ancient or modern, that have been attempted in this way.' Unfortunately, no examples of this kind of work seem to have survived. However, despite the *Art-Journal*'s remarks, similar baskets of flowers were made about the same time by the Royal Pottery at Weston-super-Mare, and an engraving in Llewellynn Jewitt's *Ceramic Art of Great Britain* gives some idea of their appearance.

During the 'seventies Watcombe continued to extend the range of its products, and the classical-type vases, of which the reproduction of the Portland Vase shown in Fig. 5 is a good example, were compared favourably with Wedgwood jasper-ware. The busts of contemporary politicians, sportsmen, and royalty also proved to be very popular, as were copies of other works by Victorian sculptors. A typical example is the bust of John Bright, the Corn Law reformer, by A. Bentley, shown in Fig. 6. Other articles of a similar nature were portrait medallions intended to be set into a wall, such as the roundel of Fig. 7 with a cherub's face in high relief.

Most of the early Watcombe figures were of classical subjects and, like the vases, were slip-cast in plaster moulds (Fig. 8). Occasionally, however, the firm must have produced figures from plastic clay, for the Exeter Museum possesses a terracotta model of a boar, bearing the Watcombe mark, which appears to have been formed by pressing clay into a mould by hand. It is not certain, though, whether any of the originals from which the plaster moulds were taken were modelled on the premises, or whether they were supplied by outside modellers and sculptors. It is also surprising that few individually hand-modelled articles appear to have been made, apart from the early flower compositions. The portrait plaque of Mr Brock shown in Plate II, modelled by J.M. Mohr, may be an exception, but this was obviously a specially commissioned work from an independent sculptor. Certainly, some of the Pottery workers were described as 'modellers', but this description was applied to men who assembled the separate parts of a figure after they came out of the moulds. The moulds themselves would usually have been made from suitably scaled copies of the originals. These were presumably supplied with the permission of the artist in the case of contemporary sculptors; whilst there were, no doubt, studios elsewhere equipped to produce copies of classical works.

Nevertheless, the Pottery was not above copying the current models of other firms, as is shown by the existence of a figure of a boy on skates, found both in plain terracotta and decorated with coloured enamels (Fig. 9). This is obviously based on 'Winter', from a set of figures representing the four Seasons made by the Derby china factory (and previously at Bristol), although Watcombe does not seem to have made any of the three companion figures. Another instance, apparently, of direct copying is the small font (?) in the form of a kneeling angel holding a shell, shown in Fig. 10. This has been photographed by the side of a version in parian porcelain made by Byng and Grondahl of Copenhagen. Since the terracotta figure is slightly smaller than the porcelain article, and noticeably less detailed, it was almost certainly cast from a mould taken directly from the latter, the reduction in size being due to normal shrinkage during the subsequent processing.

Despite Watcombe's preference in the 'seventies for copying

existing works, some models intended for production in quantity were evidently specially commissioned by the firm, for a bust of Princess Louise in the Exeter Museum carries the following moulded inscription on the reverse:

'The Watcombe Terra-Cotta Clay Co. Ltd; Watcombe, Torquay, Proprietors. Published March 1879. Modelled expressly for the Company by LIEFCHILD.'

Other articles had their title, or the name of the original artist, moulded in a conspicuous position; with the Pottery mark under the base, but many of the very early Watcombe pieces have no mark of any kind. This is presumably because the quality of the terracotta itself was considered to be sufficient identification until the advent of rival potteries in the district. When a mark was applied it usually consisted of the words 'WATCOMBE/TORQUAY' impressed or transfer-printed in black, although from about 1875 a complicated circular printed mark, incorporating a woodpecker on a tree, was sometimes used.

Enamel Decoration

Towards the end of the 'seventies the more severe styles of the early Watcombe wares were beginning to lose popularity in face of the newer forms of Art pottery being developed elsewhere. This led to the introduction of a few new terracotta models, including several teapots in a pseudo-Japanese style. But the shapes of the firm's products were determined by the large number of moulds that had been prepared and it was easier, at least as an interim measure, to adopt new styles of decoration than to change the shapes.

One type of decoration that had already been introduced by Mr Brock in the mid-'seventies consisted of a kind of fresco painting on thin clay plaques. This involved the application of coloured slips to a raw clay panel and then fixing the design in a single firing. Alternatively, a vase or plaque might be made from a light-coloured clay and then dipped in slip of a darker shade. When nearly dry the outer layer was partially scraped or carved away to create the pattern. A further variation of this procedure was to carve a design on a pot and then decorate the areas in relief with coloured enamels, as in the case of the Egyptian style vase shown in Fig. 4. Examples of free-hand sgraffito decoration are also occasionally found, depicting animals or other subjects, which appear to be imitations of the kind of work done by some of the Doulton stoneware artists.

Another development was the extension of the earlier practice of enamelling simple borders and motifs to include the decoration of vases and plaques with studies of birds, flowers, and foliage, done in a natural manner and in realistic colours (Fig. 11). The decoration was applied to the article while it was in the biscuit condition, and then fired-on in an enamelling oven. In the 'seventies a favourite subject for enamel decoration was the globular type of water bottle with a long tapering neck, and such articles were often given a band of small flowers and leaves round the centre of the body. During the 'eighties, however, the shape of vase known as a 'pilgrim flask' became very popular. This had flat circular sides that formed ideal panels for more elaborate treatment by an artist. The technique was also employed to produce open sprays of leaves and flowers trailing over the surface of a vase.

At the end of the 'seventies Watcombe had probably reached the peak of its popularity. By this time the firm had established world-wide markets, and its products were regularly shipped as far away as America and Australia. It was also a frequent exhibitor at the numerous International Exhibitions, both at home and abroad, that were such a feature of commercial life during the second half of the nineteenth century. Some of the newer styles of decoration were shown at the Paris International Exhibition of 1878 and subsequently illustrated in the catalogue published by the *Art-Journal*. Allowing for the fact that exhibitors at these shows tended to present their best and most ornate products, it is noteworthy that several of the Watcombe articles in the 1878 Exhibition were elaborately decorated and wholly or partly glazed. The *Pottery Gazette*'s notice of this event mentioned, in particular, a plaque painted underglaze with begonias; while several vases with painted decoration in panels, which would previously have had their feet and necks left as plain terracotta, were now given an overall clear glaze.

These glazed wares were evidently an attempt to compete with the major china manufacturers and some of them, at least, were given the printed mark: 'WATCOMBE/PORCELAIN'. The exact significance of this description is not known, as such marks are now rare. The use of the word 'porcelain' suggests that articles of this type were fired at a higher temperature than ordinary terracotta, and some examples certainly have a darker appearance than would be due simply to the glaze (Fig. 29). The description can hardly have been adopted as a distinguishing name for the complete range of glazed wares, since other glazed articles, such as ornate jardinieres, can be found with the more usual Watcombe marks.

The Watcombe Works

About the Pottery itself during this first period very little has been recorded, and it almost seems as if the inhabitants of Torquay, although proud of the local terracotta, were slightly ashamed of having anything so commercial as a factory on their doorstep. The Works by the side of the Teignmouth Road employed nearly a hundred people, and six kilns were in regular use; no doubt producing a considerable volume of smoke when lighting-up. There was also an eighty-foot chimney for the boiler of the steam-driven machinery. The buildings themselves were slate-roofed and set round a central yard in the middle of a field, originally of rough grass. In the course of time, though, the Works became surrounded with additional clay pits, weathering tanks, and water pumps — not a very picturesque sight, and probably the reason why no adequate photographs exist of the Pottery (Fig. 12).

Soon after the construction of the Pottery Mr Brock had built himself a house on the corner of the Teignmouth Road and what is now Pavor Road, overlooking the grounds of the factory. The rear wall of this house was decorated with a large bas-relief terracotta panel (Fig. 13) and was named, appropriately enough, 'Etruscan Lodge'. Although some distance from the Works, it is recalled that Mr Brock, who had a very powerful voice, was in the habit of leaning out of an upstairs side window and shouting the name of a girl who worked in the packing shed. This unfortunate individual would then have to leave her work and come running up the drive to take a message.

Originally, the showroom was just part of the packing shed. However, at a later date a more attractive building was erected, for the convenience of visitors, at the entrance to the drive that led down to the Works from the main road.

In the early 'eighties, despite its apparent prosperity, the Watcombe Terra-Cotta Clay Company found itself in difficulties. These were probably due mainly to the trade depression of the period, but another factor must have been the death of Mr Allen in the mid-'seventies, which had deprived the firm of its founder. Also, Mr Brock seems to have left by 1882, for the local directory of that year gave a Mr Samuel Stonier as Manager of the Pottery, and his address as Etruscan Lodge. Faced with a large stock of unsold wares the remaining directors therefore decided to dispose of the business, and the Works were closed down some time in 1883. Although there was no reference to this event in the trade journals, it is significant that the firm's regular advertisements in the *Pottery Gazette* were suddenly discontinued, and it was not until March of 1884 that the same periodical noted, without comment, that the 'Watcombe Terra-Cotta Company' had resumed operations.

Fig. ii. Unusual glazed Watcombe vase with a buff body, decorated by carving away an outer coating of coffee-coloured slip. Probably c. 1880. Mark: No. 2. Height: 330 mm (13.0 in).

2.2. THE WATCOMBE POTTERY

When the Watcombe Works were reopened in 1884 they had been acquired by new proprietors — Evans and Company — in whose hands they remained until the end of the century. Mr Evans lived in the Ellacombe district of Torquay and took an active part in the day-to-day running of the Pottery. Unfortunately, many of the best craftsmen of the Brock period had by then left to set up small potteries of their own, probably from sheer financial necessity, and never returned to the parent firm. These circumstances, combined with the dictates of fashion, accelerated a change in the character of the Watcombe wares which had begun even before 1880 and continued until the late 'nineties. This change was emphasized by the dropping of the words 'Terra-Cotta Clay' from the official name of the firm, which was now called simply 'The Watcombe Pottery Company', with the subsidiary description 'Fine Art Potters'.

This second phase of the Pottery's existence was marked by a gradual abandonment of classical shapes and restrained decoration in favour of what can only be described as an amalgam of typical late Victorian styles. Mr Snowden Ward, writing in the *Art-Journal* in 1900, recalled that the original firm had made a 'strong and well-sustained' effort to produce classical subjects, but the results were not as satisfactory as had been hoped and the demand did not fill the extensive workshops erected for their manufacture. Nevertheless, the firm continued to produce terracotta figures, busts, and plaques, but with the emphasis now on contemporary subjects. These included plant pots, spill vases, and other ornaments, often disguised by figures in costume of the period, such as the paper-boy of Fig. 14; and free-standing statuettes, of which the 'Whistling Coon' (Fig. 15) is a typical example.

Another market for terracotta in the 'eighties and 'nineties was the supply of statuettes and other articles for advertising purposes, and Mr Ward implied that these were made in even greater numbers than pieces intended for sale in the ordinary way. The best-known of the advertising figures was the group associated with Pears' soap, known as 'You Dirty Boy' (Fig. 16). This depicted an old woman scrubbing a small boy over a tub of water, and was originally modelled by the Italian sculptor G. Focardi. After being shown at the Paris Exhibition of 1878 (where it was awarded a prize) reduced copies were made at Watcombe right up to the time of the Great War, over thirty separately moulded pieces being assembled to form the complete article.

Oil Painting

The new proprietors of the Watcombe Pottery also introduced painting in oils as a means of providing bright and cheerful decoration in the current taste to maintain the demand for terracotta vases and other articles formed in the existing moulds. Compared with enamel decoration, oil painting was not only simpler, cheaper, and quicker, but it did not need to be fired afterwards and the range of colours was virtually unlimited. This ware, according to Mr Ward, was:

'. . . . mostly sold at a very low rate to that section of the public which admires classic shapes, "hand-painted" and purchasable for a few pence. To meet the same sort of demand, great plaques of terracotta, painted with large and brilliant chrysanthemums, poppies, and other flowers that lend themselves to much show for little labour, are also produced and are hugely popular. To certain givers of presents a "hand-painted" plaque, about the size of a cart-wheel, which can be bought for three or four shillings,* proves very attractive.'

Admittedly, Mr Ward's disparaging remarks may have been justified in the case of small articles, where the decoration tended to be perfunctory. However, the larger vases and plaques were competently painted, even when the subjects were of a routine nature, and are often charmingly decorative. Nevertheless, oil painting is a relatively impermanent form of decoration on pottery, compared with fired work, and difficult to clean.

Compositions of flowers were the favourite subject for oil decoration, and plaques were sometimes offered in sets of four, representing the Seasons. These plaques were produced both in circular and oval shapes, often with a moulded rim to represent a picture frame, and the painted area was often lightly varnished as a protection against Victorian smoke and grime. Colourful birds were also very popular (Fig. 17), followed by marine views, landscapes and, occasionally, figures of children in Kate Greenaway style (Fig. 18). All the decorating at this time was done by men, but it should be remembered that the firm also sold terracotta blanks to suppliers of artists' materials, and plaques bearing the Watcombe impressed mark need not necessarily have been painted in the Works.

Painting on ceramic plaques, both by professionals and amateurs, had been introduced at Minton's Kensington Studios in the early 'seventies. It was further popularized by Howell and James, the Regent Street dealers, who held regular competitions and exhibitions of amateur work, the vogue persisting as a fashionable pastime for ladies until the end of the century. Amateur work is often signed but, as might be expected, the quality is very variable. It is most unusual, however, to find articles of Watcombe pottery signed by a decorator known to have been employed at the factory, and the firm does not seem to have encouraged the practice. Fig. 19 shows a plaque of very fine quality painted and signed by

*The original price of a terracotta article will often be found written underneath it — the material accepted a pencil so well that there was no need for a label.

Holland Birbeck (the son of William Birbeck, the Coalport and Copeland decorator) who worked at various times for both the Watcombe and Torquay Terra-Cotta companies at the end of the nineteenth century. But even this could have been done by the artist privately on a blank obtained from the Pottery. Occasionally, the initials of other decorators are found on articles, but at the time of writing their identities remain conjectural.

Early Underglaze Decoration

Although an example of underglaze decorated pottery had been shown at the Paris Exhibition of 1878, it was not until the mid-'eighties that this technique was regularly practiced at Watcombe. It had the advantage of being more controllable than enamel painting, and it also enabled the firm to compete with established china manufacturers, such as Minton and Coalport, in the production of highly decorated wares.

When Mr Evans first took over the Watcombe Pottery it seems that some early classical-type vases were 'dressed-up' with floral decoration in the contemporary manner and then glazed, probably as an additional means of disposing of old and otherwise unsaleable stock. Fig. 20, for example, shows one of a pair of remarkable vases from this transitional period which are profusely decorated with all the fashionable floral emblems of the Aesthetic movement, including sunflowers and lilies, done in a combination of thick coloured slips and pigments. As if this were not enough, the background has been stippled with slip to produce a rough surface, while the necks and bases are painted to resemble marble!

By the late 'eighties, however, more suitable shapes for underglaze decoration were introduced, mostly of Oriental derivation. The best Watcombe examples of this kind of work were produced in the last decade of the century and were done by painting on to the article while in the biscuit state, either directly on the red body or over a thin ground of white slip. Although the latter method gave the better rendering of colours, it could just as well have been applied to an article of white clay since, apart from the base and the interior, it completely obscured the fine red body. The subjects of this style of decoration were often very colourful, and included exotic birds, flowers, and fish. After painting, the article was given a colourless glaze and sometimes finished with bright gilding round the neck and foot, and on the handles (Fig. 21).

Thrown Wares

Faced with a continuing decline in the demand for terracotta during the 1890s, the proprietors decided to introduce a simpler and cheaper range of glazed wares, of the type that had been made at the Aller Vale Pottery since the mid-'eighties. Some of the space in the Watcombe Works, previously allocated to moulding, was therefore fitted out with potters' wheels and local craftsmen were taught the art of throwing by experts from London and Staffordshire. Even so, the firm was anxious not to lower its traditional high standards of craftsmanship and would not use power-driven wheels, preferring to adopt the old type of 'string wheel' that was operated with a rope belt driven by an assistant turning a handle.

Although Watcombe was reluctant to introduce throwing, it did enable the firm to produce true Art pottery according to William Morris's definitions (see p.28). As a result the underglaze-decorated vases from the late 'nineties were usually thrown, rather than moulded, but the better-quality examples were still turned on the outside to provide a smooth surface for the decorator. Unfortunately, the cost of producing the more ornate examples was by then making them unprofitable, and in 1900 it was announced that they were being discontinued.

The new styles of thrown pottery introduced in the late 'nineties were generally smaller than the earlier wares, and obviously aimed at a cheaper market. One of the first ventures in this direction was a range of articles, called 'Green-and-Straw' ware, consisting of vases and jugs of almost rustic appearance that were made entirely from white clay (Fig. 96). A decorative effect was imparted by applying translucent green glaze, usually to the upper part of each article only, and allowing it to run down in streaks to blend with the clear glaze on the lower part. The vases were sometimes provided with impracticable peaked handles, and both vases and jugs might be dimpled to enhance the rustic effect. Another range of small ornamental pieces, described as 'Egyptian' ware, was introduced in 1900; but it did not catch on, and examples are now very rare. The articles were decorated with appropriate motifs, such as the outlines of scarab beetles, scratched through the white slip ground to show the red body underneath (Fig. 22).

With the general introduction of simple glazed pottery the manufacture of terracotta was not suddenly discontinued, although it gradually became less popular. Much of this late terracotta consisted of cheap, slip-cast, ornaments painted with a few nondescript white flowers (Fig. 82). Because of their irregular shapes these could not be given a turned finish and, as a result, they have a rough surface and poor appearance, quite unlike the substantial terracotta articles of the 'seventies and 'eighties.

White Clay Wares

During the last decade of the century the Watcombe Pottery had been experimenting with the use of white clay for a variety of articles, apart from the Green-and-Straw ware, that were usually finished in coloured translucent glazes. One example, illustrated in Fig. 23, is the hanging jardiniere with three ring handles and a glaze that shades from red at the top to a streaky sea-green at the bottom. Another is the posy-holder, in the form of a girl hauling-in a fishing net, shown in Fig. 24. This typical late-Victorian ornament is moulded from white clay and tinted with glazes of various colours in the style of mid-nineteenth century Staffordshire majolica. It was undoubtedly paired, originally, with a corresponding figure of a boy. Mention should also be made of a range of wares which were finished with splashed multi-coloured glazes to resemble marble, although these had a red terracotta body.

These colour-glaze effects were evidently produced to satisfy the contemporary demand for 'Art faience', for which some of the Midland and Northern potteries, such as Ault and Burmantofts, were noted. In complete contrast is the white terracotta plate shown in Fig. 25, which is moulded all over with an arabesque design picked out in coloured oil paints.

Yet another activity of the Watcombe Pottery in the 'nineties that involved white ware was the decoration of china table services 'imported' from Staffordshire. Although this was probably not a stock line and done to special order, several part services have been noted, hand-painted with scenic views or flowers and carrying the transfer-printed woodpecker mark. These have always been of white bone china impressed with the name 'BROWNFIELD' (a Cobridge firm), and the decoration is sometimes signed by a member of the Birbeck family.

2.3. THE ROYAL WATCOMBE POTTERIES

The conversion of the Watcombe Pottery to the production of 'popular' wares was accelerated in 1901, when the business was acquired by Hexter, Humpherson and Company. This firm had for many years operated a pottery at Kingsteignton for the manufacture of tiles and sanitary goods from the white clay of the Teign valley, and in 1897 it had bought the Aller Vale Pottery, between Torquay and Newton Abbot. The full name of the new combine was 'The Royal Aller Vale and Watcombe Art Potteries',* the 'Royal' being intended to emphasize that Aller Vale had enjoyed the patronage of members of the Royal Family. However, the firm was generally referred to by its employees during the twentieth century as 'The Royal Watcombe Potteries' for short. As far as the St. Marychurch Works were concerned the business seems to have been run by the Hexter family, and it is still recalled how the 'young Hexters' used to arrive each day in a pony trap from Newton Abbot.

Edwardian Styles

The new owners probably hoped to 'rationalize' the activities of the two potteries (to use a modern phrase) in order to secure the larger, and international, markets built up by Watcombe

*This is believed to be the correct version of the name, but several variants can be found in directories and advertisements.

for the Aller-type wares. These were mainly small ornamental articles made from red clay, decorated with standard designs done in coloured slips and always highly glazed. Not only did Watcombe start making pottery with typical Aller shapes and patterns in the first decade of the present century, but it used the same pattern numbers to identify them. As a result it is often difficult, in the absence of factory marks, to distinguish articles made in the one Pottery from their counterparts made in the other. In such cases it is helpful to remember that Watcombe 'popular' wares of the first quarter of the present century can often be identified by their handles, which are usually pressed into the shape of a leaf at both ends. Aller Vale handles are only occasionally shaped in this way (mainly on traditional style articles); while at Longpark, which was the only other Pottery to shape its handle ends, the leaf impression was sometimes raised on a pad, like a wax seal.

One of the Aller specialities adopted by Watcombe was the Motto Ware, which had little aphorisms scratched through the cream-coloured ground to show up in the red clay of the body. Such articles were usually decorated, in addition, with coloured slip designs of the 'Scandy' type. Alternatively the mottoes were sometimes written in thick white slip, like icing sugar on a cake, on a dark green ground (Fig. 26). At a rather later date, about the time of the Great War, a style of decoration showing a thatched cottage between trees, done in a combination of scratch-work and coloured slips, was introduced as an alternative to Scandy (Fig. 27). This was called 'Devon Motto Ware', and often marked as such on the base, although it is now generally known as 'Cottage Ware'. Watcombe was not the first of the local potteries to introduce slip-painted cottages as a decorative pattern, for the Brewers were using this subject before 1905. Nevertheless, other firms were quick to follow Watcombe, and the Cottage motif is now generally thought of before anything else as typical of Torquay pottery.

Another characteristic of the Cottage Ware was that it was often inscribed, in addition to a motto, with the name of the place where it would be sold. The names usually found are those of South Coast seaside resorts, but names of towns throughout the British Isles were incised on consignments intended for the appropriate localities.

Apart from the Motto Ware with its stylized decoration, Watcombe also continued the type of naturalistic slip decoration introduced by Aller Vale in the 'nineties. Some of this work was very competently done, and the vase shown in Fig. 28, with its fish swimming under a thick 'wet' glaze, could almost be mistaken for a product of the Brannam Pottery at Barnstaple. Other articles, such as jardinieres with lilies painted in pale greens and white on a dark green ground, or yellow daffodils on a tall jug, are equally charming but of a more routine nature.

The normal factory mark on Watcombe pottery in the decade before the Great War was 'WATCOMBE/TORQUAY' impressed in rather irregular block capitals and quite different from the smaller and neater nineteenth century version. A possible reason for the rough appearance of the Edwardian mark is that it was applied, not with a metal tool, but with a stamp made from terracotta. These stamps were made by pressing the end of a wedge-shaped piece of clay into an engraved die and then firing it. The pattern number, however, continued to be scratched on the base of an article with whatever tool happened to be at hand; usually, it is said, a sharpened six-inch nail.

The combination of dark green grounds or borders with a dark body imparted a rather sombre appearance to much of the Watcombe pottery of the Edwardian period. Although the green was a matter of fashion, the body colour was not always the effect of the glaze, or the result of harder firing. By this time the original bed of light-coloured material near Watcombe House had been worked out, and clay had to be obtained by digging in the fields surrounding the Pottery, or wherever else it could be found. Occasionally, the firm was offered seams of clay that had been uncovered during local building operations. Someone would then have to go out to the site and test the clay for plasticity and smoothness. The former quality was assessed by kneading the clay with the hands, and the latter by chewing a lump; the only essential item of equipment carried by the tester being a bottle of water to wash out his mouth afterwards!

Faience Decoration

By the second decade of the present century there was a renewed interest amongst the Torquay potteries in underglaze painted decoration, using conventional pigment colours on a white or cream-coloured ground, but of a much simpler type than the Victorian work. It is convenient to distinguish this type of pottery as Faience since, although it was not done on a tin oxide ground as in olden times, the process was essentially the same as that employed by Doulton's for their celebrated 'Lambeth Faience' of the late nineteenth century. At the Torquay potteries the earlier slip decoration had been restricted, by its very nature, to relatively broad designs done in coloured liquid clays that left a slightly raised surface. The pigment decoration, however, left a smooth surface and could be used for more detailed work in a wider range of colours. Another point worth noting is that the twentieth-century glaze, being colourless and presumably lead-free, did not impart the yellowish cast seen on some of the wares made in the nineteenth century. Nevertheless, the faience painting did not supplant slip decoration, and both techniques continued to be used until well into the 1930s, and even later.

Just before the Great War several characteristic subjects for underglaze decoration were introduced at Watcombe. Of these, three are particularly associated with this Pottery: 'Marine Views' (as they were advertised), flowers, and scenes of topographic interest. The marine views depicted brown-sailed fishing vessels, usually Brixham yawls, in a calm estuary against a yellow evening sky with a distant landscape of trees and houses. Fig. 30 shows a biscuit barrel decorated in this way with a scene that runs continuously round the article and joins up on itself. What is not obvious from the photograph is that the shaded background tones, such as the sky, were obtained by using a small spray-gun, of the type known as an 'air brush', while the article was rotated on a banding wheel.*

---

*At about this time the Aller Vale/Watcombe combine was also producing articles decorated with sailing boats done in slip, with brown fore-and-aft sails, a single mast, and a black hull. But in comparison with the faience their painting is rudimentary, and they were probably done simply to emulate the slip-painted boats of the Longpark Pottery.

The flower subjects, which continued to be popular into the 'twenties, usually consisted of boldly outlined sprays of two or three blooms with surrounding foliage. Before the War these were usually painted direct on to the white ground, although later examples were often done with a streaky mauve or magenta ground brushed over the basic white dip. Fig. 31 shows examples of both types: a jug and a vase painted with blue clematis flowers and a small plate with wild roses. It is interesting to note that the jug has the same shape and is incised with the same shape number (885) as the Aller Vale slip-decorated jug of Fig. 88 that was made some fifteen years earlier. However, in common with the practice on all Watcombe faience-type work, there is no number marked on the article to identify the pattern of the decoration.

The topographic painting usually depicted named landmarks or beauty spots in various parts of the country; the articles so decorated being intended for sale in the appropriate localities (Fig. 32). They were generally finished with sprayed green borders; but the decoration, although assured, has a mechanical quality which must have been at least partly due to the monotonous nature of such repetition work.

Apart from the three main classes of faience painting just mentioned, other subjects are often encountered. Amongst them are birds (Fig. 33), including copies of the Longpark Cockerel patterns, cottages, windmills, and fruit. Although many examples suffer from the same stiffness of drawing and hard gradation of tones as the landscapes, some small figures of birds are quite charming, even if they bear no comparison with the underglaze work of the late nineteenth century.

Yet another kind of finish introduced about 1915 was that applied to a range of pottery described as 'Art Green Ware'. This was simply a translucent green glaze applied to various articles of relatively simple shapes, either directly over a red or brown body or, more often, over articles which had previously been partly or wholly coated with white slip. When correctly processed, the glaze acquired an iridescence resembling that of the well-known green-glaze ware of the Farnham Pottery in Surrey. Three examples of Watcombe Art Green Ware are shown in Fig. 34, including a bowl with owl faces that was also copied from the bird jugs made at Farnham.

E

The Inter-War Period

The types of articles made at Watcombe during the first quarter of the present century were very varied. Apart from the small jugs, vases, and tea-services of Aller Vale origin the firm produced a wide range of useful and ornamental wares; including ink bottles and stands, toast racks, plaques (Fig. 35), ash-trays, and jardinieres with their matching pedestals. Many of these, like the popular 1476 pattern tea-service, continued to have the old Aller pattern numbers scratched on them after the merger of the two firms. Even the occasional pieces of terracotta were still being made in the 'twenties from the old moulds. Some new shapes were introduced at this time, but they were not usually marked with a pattern number, probably because impressed and incised marks were being abandoned in favour of simpler rubber-stamped factory marks. In addition to articles sold through normal channels, the Pottery had a substantial business making undecorated articles under contract. These included deodorizers, and liners for silver cache-pots; but such things are unlikely to be of much interest to the collector.

In the early 'twenties Watcombe introduced a range of articles decorated with Egyptian scenes, probably inspired by contemporary archaeological discoveries in that country. These were painted underglaze with sailing boats, palm trees, pyramids, and figures against a predominantly yellow foreground and blue sky. But the most characteristic styles of decoration introduced between the Wars involved underglaze painting, mainly in pigment colours, on an overall bright blue ground. The best-known pattern, which Watcombe claimed to have originated and is said to have been devised by a Mr Hunt in the mid-'twenties, is the 'Kingfisher' design. This shows a kingfisher, painted in natural colours, diving into a pool containing water-lilies and rushes. Some of the better examples, such as the small ash-tray shown in Fig. 36, are very attractive, the blue ground covering the whole of the outer surface and set off by a black rim or handle. Alternatively, a stork was sometimes painted on tall vases, but this is much less common.

The Kingfisher pattern was copied by several other Torquay potteries, chiefly Longpark, and the bright blue ground is typical of much of the local ware of the inter-War period. Fig. 37, for example, shows two blue-ground bowls, decorated with a jazz pattern of bright colours that probably represents Watcombe's nearest approach to 'Art Deco', together with a small *pot-pourri* jar painted with a geometrical design. Also included in the photograph is a teapot decorated with figures moulded in low relief and picked out in colours; rather like some Staffordshire copper-lustre teapots of a century earlier, except that the blue ground takes the place of the lustre.

Another innovation of the late 'twenties or early 'thirties was the use of semi-matt glazes of the type associated with the Poole Pottery (Carter, Stabler & Adams Ltd). Fig. 38 shows a striking quart-size jug of this period finished with streaked matt glazes in a variety of bright colours, including orange, green, and blue. Articles were also decorated by spraying through patterned stencils to give a soft-outline effect on a thin white ground with an eggshell finish.

During the inter-War period, though, and for the remainder of Watcombe's existence, the Cottage Ware was the bread-and-butter product that kept the Pottery going. Surprisingly it was the mottoes that sold the ware, and it has been said: "If you had left off the writing you wouldn't have had a factory." As with Aller Vale pottery, there is a widely held belief that the early inscriptions were in plain English, and that the later ones were in Devon dialect to make the articles more attractive to the average tourist. However, this is not entirely true since, apart from articles destined for specific markets such as Scotland, the little proverbs and 'cute sayings' were selected more or less at random from a book, kept in the showroom, in which visitors were invited to enter mottoes of their own for use by the Pottery. In the course of time a great many visitors' books were accumulated, but they were all destroyed when the Works were demolished. The variety of mottoes encountered is seemingly endless, but a selection will be found in Appendix IV.

The Watcombe Families

Although the *Art-Journal* had referred to the employment of women and girls at Watcombe in 1872, they were then only engaged in unskilled work and in the warehouse. Until the Great War all the decorators were men, and even after the War the better-quality painting was still done by male artists. But women came into the Pottery during the War and they remained afterwards to decorate the Cottage, Motto, and other popular wares.

By this time we are within the range of living memory and the names of the artists of the inter-War period are still familiar in St. Marychurch. They included: Harry Crute, Henry Birbeck (the son of Holland Birbeck, and generally known as Harry), the Wilsons (father and son), a Mr Barker, and Mr Hunt of Kingfisher fame. These men, like china decorators elsewhere, seem to have been in the habit of 'moving around' from one firm to another and Harry Crute, whose name always crops up in any talk of the old Torquay potteries, ran a small business of his own — called the Daison Pottery — for a time between the Wars (see Sect. 6).

Throughout its existence, the Watcombe Pottery served as a reservoir of talent for the local industry. Many an enterprising employee left the firm to branch out on his own; and not a few returned to the fold when times became hard outside. As Mr Arthur Cole, the former manager, once said: "as long as he wasn't mixed up with the glazing, you didn't mind anyone leaving and going to another Pottery." Another characteristic of the firm was that, even if it was not a family business, it was very much a business of families, since many of its employees were members of a few large families who had worked in the Pottery all their lives. The Coles, for example, served the company for over ninety years, and provided three generations of managers. There were also the Clements — Fred, Eddie and Ernie — who were handlers and wedgers; Fred and Sid Dart, who threw all the large pieces, and 'four or five' Bradford brothers who were decorators and had come over to Watcombe when Aller Vale closed down. Other names of this period included the Hicks brothers and Charlie Annan, who were turners; and John Stevenson, who was chiefly a modeller (Fig. 39).

Because of this family tradition, and the fact that Hexter, Humpherson paid slightly higher wages than other firms in Torquay, staff relationships were generally good. Except, that is, when the men played football in the yard during the dinner hour and ended up by breaking a window. Then the manager would rush out of his office shouting "never again" and football would be banned — for a time!

Nevertheless, it was not an easy life in the Torquay potteries. At the outbreak of war in 1914 the hours were from 6.30 in the morning until 6 at night, with half an hour for breakfast and an hour for dinner. The Watcombe Pottery was lit by gas from the Barton Gas Works, mostly with open-flame burners, and there was also a gas engine to drive some of the machinery. In the winter those workers who needed a good light, such as the decorators and the turners, would drill holes in the piping and light the escaping gas, not only for the extra illumination, but also to scare away the rats! Yet a boy just out of school would be pleased to start at the Pottery for 7/6d a week, rising to half a sovereign (paid in gold) in his mid-teens; for jobs were hard to find and the only alternative was employment on a farm or in one of the local marble Works.

The Final Years

Watcombe had always had an international market for its wares. It was therefore able to obtain an export licence during the Second World War, and so remained in production when other Torquay potteries, such as Longpark, had to close 'for the duration'. After the War the Pottery was faced with the need to reorganize itself and rationalize its products to meet the changed economic circumstances. The proprietors therefore decided to transfer the business to the associated Mid-Devon Trading Company, which also acquired and reopened the Longpark Pottery.

In this way the new owners obtained a virtual monopoly of the red clay pottery industry in South Devon. Unfortunately, the demand for this kind of ware had fallen, and the cost of labour had risen, to the extent that the more elaborate styles of decoration were becoming too expensive for the market. During the decade following the War a number of new and simpler styles were therefore introduced. These included the 'Polka Dot' pattern (inspired by a dress worn by Princess Margaret when she visited the Pottery), and variants of the Cottage and Motto wares in rather brighter colours and glossier finish than formerly (Fig. 40).

In 1957, in an attempt to reduce costs still further, the Pottery was converted at considerable expense to electric firing. At the same time the 80-foot chimney, which had dominated the Works for nearly a century, was demolished. This event was regarded by many of the employees as an ill omen, as indeed it proved to be. The proprietors then engaged the services of a consultant from Staffordshire to advise on a complete review of the Pottery's activities. It seems that the advice contained the recommendation that the firm should introduce a range of white earthenwares, including kitchen and oven ware, to enable it to compete in a wider market. Although this proposal was resisted by some of the older members of the staff, on the grounds that white and red clay pottery could not be produced side by side in one factory, experimental production was commenced of white kitchen-ware decorated with a blue glaze. However, a great deal of trouble was experienced with the glaze flaking off, presumably owing to lack of familiarity with the materials. Various ornamental articles were also introduced in the white body, and Fig. 41 shows one of the last types of vase made at Watcombe. This is finished in an eggshell black glaze and decorated with a repetitive incised design that shows up in white against the dark ground. Nevertheless, although quite effective in the right setting, it was not what most people expected from the Watcombe Pottery.

Whether these uncharacteristic products would eventually have given the firm a new lease of life is doubtful. The question is, in any case, only of academic interest now because, in March 1962, the Mid-Devon Trading Co. decided to close the Works and sell the site to the South-Western Electricity Supply Board for a maintenance depot. Although there were large orders outstanding, notices were given out to the staff, the Pottery was shut down in November, and the buildings demolished in 1963. The manager was given instructions to 'get rid of everything' and all the old moulds, the glazes and, apparently, the firm's records, were buried in a clay pit. Many of the old pieces of terracotta were sold to a china retailer, while a tile panel of a potter at his wheel which decorated the showroom is said to have been acquired by the Fulham Pottery. But the plaques of W.G. Grace and other Victorian worthies that adorned the outside walls of the buildings were just bulldozed away, and at the time of writing the showroom alone still stands at the side of the Teignmouth Road as a reminder of the achievements of the Royal Watcombe Potteries.

WATCOMBE MARKS

(i) *Factory Marks.* Very early (i.e. pre-1875) Watcombe terracotta was often unmarked. After about 1875 most, but not all, terracotta was given a factory mark. From 1901 onwards it was normal practice to mark all wares, although some articles escaped marking.

1.	**WATCOMBE TORQUAY**	Early impressed mark. The letters have serifs. c.1871— c.1875.
2.	WATCOMBE TORQUAY	The standard 19th century mark, usually impressed in small, neat, sanserif letters. Also found as black transfer-printed lettering. c.1871— 1901.
3.	**W**	Impressed mark found on small articles, c.1875—c.1883.
4.	WATCOMBE TORQUAY	The curved version of 2. Usually found on vases or small articles. Always impressed. c.1880—1901.

5.

Early version of the 'Wood-pecker' mark, transfer-printed on terracotta, c.1875—1883. Impressed c.1875—c.1895.

6.

Later, and smaller, version of the 'Woodpecker' mark, transfer-printed and used by Evans & Co. on glazed wares. 1884—1901.

7. WATCOMBE
    TORQUAY

This impressed mark, with irregular lettering, is found on early 20th century glazed pottery. It should not be confused with the smaller and neater 19th century mark (No.2). 1901—c.1920; occasionally, with 'ENGLAND' added, until c.1930.

8. *Watcombe*
    Torquay
    England

Broadly incised or painted mark on glazed wares of better-average quality. 'Torquay' and/or 'England' may be omitted. 1st quarter, 20th century.

9.

Early, rubber-stamped, under-glaze mark. Seldom found. c.1915.

10. WATCOMBE
     PORCELAIN

Rare printed mark, found on some glazed terracotta articles, c.1878—1883(?).

11.   **Watcombe Torquay**   Impressed mark, in lower-case lettering; often associated with 'Made in England' stamped in similar characters. c.1915—c.1920.

12.

WATCOMBE
TORQUAY
MADE IN
ENGLAND

Impressed mark with irregular lettering. c.1920—c.1927.

13.

WATCOMBE

DEVON
MOTTO
WARE
REG: No.
B 664776

ENGLAND

Rubber-stamped mark applied to articles decorated with cottages and mottoes. c.1918 —? The Registered Number is sometimes omitted.

14.

**WATCOMBE
TORQUAY
ENGLAND**

Black rubber-stamped mark, c.1928—c.1945.

15.

ROYAL
WATCOMBE
TORQUAY
ENGLAND

Late rubber-stamped mark, in black or cream. c.1945—1962.

(ii) *Turners' Marks.* Most Watcombe terracotta with a turned finish was impressed by the turner with his personal stamp. In the absence of a factory mark these stamps are useful for establishing the provenance of an article. However, it should be noted that mark No. 16(b) is also found on articles made by the Torquay Terra-Cotta Co. and may have been the stamp of a Mr Willott. In the case of slip-cast busts having a separate, bolted-on, base the turner's mark *on the base* is often the only mark on the article.

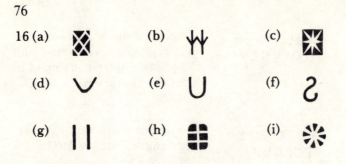

16 (a)   (b)   (c)

(d)   (e)   (f)

(g)   (h)   (i)

(iii) *Pattern Numbers*. Nineteenth century terracotta articles sometimes have impressed, painted or, occasionally, incised numbers on their bases. The impressed figures, of up to four digits, would appear to be pattern numbers denoting the shape, but identical articles have been noted with different numbers. The significance of incised numbers, of one or two digits, is not known.

Numbers, of up to four digits, painted in black in small neat characters probably refer to the style of decoration. In the absence of other marks they tend to confirm a Torquay (i.e. Watcombe or Torquay Terra-Cotta Co.) origin, since the pattern numbers on Staffordshire terracotta were often painted in white or coloured enamel.

Four-figure numbers beginning with 18 or 19 should not be interpreted as indicating the year of manufacture without additional evidence.

Glazed Watcombe pottery made during the first quarter of the twentieth century often has the shape number, and sometimes the decoration code, incised on the base. Such numbers are usually of Aller Vale origin (see Appendix III). Articles made from the late 1920s onward seldom bear any pattern number.

(iv) *Modellers', Moulders', and Decorators' Marks*. The following incised initials have been seen on terracotta articles and may either be modellers' or, in the case of articles with carved decoration, decorators' marks. Only mark 17 (f) has been identified, as the initials of John Stevenson, a modeller working at the turn of the century, although it is interesting to note that 17 (e) is similar to the early mark used by Eliza Simmance at Doulton's Lambeth Studios.

17 (a) **J.B.** (b) **H.B.** (c) **L**

(d) **S** (e) **E.S.** (f) **J.S.**

The only nineteenth century Watcombe decorator whose name is known was Holland Birbeck (died 1906). Articles decorated with flowers in oils and signed 'H. Birbeck' have been seen, but may have been painted privately on Watcombe blanks. Most, if not all, factory-decorated articles are unsigned. Articles bearing a Watcombe stamp, decorated in oils and signed, are usually the work of amateurs. No painted signatures have been seen on twentieth century pieces, but groups of enamel dots on twentieth century terracotta articles appear to identify the person applying routine decoration.

Section Three

HELE CROSS

Plate IV.   Classical style vase by the Torquay Terra-Cotta Co. One of a pair,
decorated with convolvulus and passion flowers in coloured enamels, possibly
by Holland Birbeck. Mark: No. 21. c. 1880.

3.1. THE TORQUAY TERRA-COTTA COMPANY

What leaf-fringed legend haunts about thy shape
  Of deities or mortals, or of both,
In Tempe or the dales of Arcady?

Keats: *Ode on a Grecian Urn*.

Encouraged, no doubt, by the success of the Watcombe
Pottery, a second firm was established on the northern
outskirts of Torquay in 1875 to make terracotta ware. This was
the 'Torquay Terra-Cotta Company Limited', to give it its full
and somewhat cumbrous title, and it was founded by a local
resident, Dr Gillow, who assumed the position of Chairman of
the firm. The site chosen for the new Pottery was at the
north-west corner of what is known locally as Hele cross roads,
or 'Hele Cross' for short, and three-quarters of a mile from the
Watcombe Works.

This location was probably determined by the proximity of
the Torquay Cemetery on the opposite side of the Hele Road.
No doubt Dr Gillow had often seen red earth dug up in the
cemetery and, realizing that here was another deposit of
Watcombe-type clay, acquired an adjacent plot of ground for
a terracotta Works.

Like the Watcombe Pottery, the new company committed
itself from the start to the production of high-quality work.
After declaring that the Hele Cross clay was believed to be the
best yet discovered, the prospectus continued:
  '. . . the aim and object is to improve the artistic standard

by persevering energy . . . (and) to improve year by year until they (i.e. the directors) place Terra-Cotta in its old proud position as a favoured branch of Ceramic Art, and until Devonshire productions stand unrivalled throughout Europe.'

The first building to be erected was a long single-storey workshop backing on to what is now the cemetery wall. This contained all the facilities for preparing and working the clay, which was dug from a pit in the middle of the site. By 1876 another, and more imposing, building had been completed to provide office and studio accommodation. This was on two floors and was decorated with ornamental terracotta features that had been made on the premises. These buildings were set at right angles to one another and approached by a short drive from Barton Hill Road. At the north end of the site, towards the Barton gas works, two kilns were erected; a bottle kiln for the first firing and a muffle for enamelling.

Early Wares

As manager of his new Works Dr Gillow engaged a Mr Ridgeway, whose name, despite the 'e' in the middle, suggests that he came from Staffordshire. Other key men may also have come down from the Potteries, while there is some evidence that experienced terracotta workers were attracted from Watcombe. Certainly, the articles made at Hele Cross during its early years were very similar to those produced on the Teignmouth Road. According to Llewellynn Jewitt (*Ceramic Art of Great Britain*, 1883) the products of the Torquay Terra-Cotta Company included:

'Statuettes, single figures and groups, busts, groups of animals, birds, etc; vases, ewers, bottles, jugs and tazzae; butter coolers, spill vases and other domestic appliances; plaques of various sizes, candlesticks, toilet trays, water bottles, tobacco vases, etc.'

In fact, the 'Torquay' Works seem to have made all those forms of terracotta originally produced at Watcombe, with the exception of hand-modelled flowers and, possibly, articles decorated with delicate applied mouldings. If anything, there was a rather greater proportion of useful wares, but little large-scale or architectural work. The Hele clay was certainly of a very fine texture and fired to a lighter and brighter shade than the Watcombe clay; the actual colour being variously described as 'light peach-red', or 'pale vermilion'. It was also said to be more brittle than its Watcombe counterpart.

Only two years after the establishment of the firm the *Art-Journal* was able to report:

'The company at Torquay, under the guidance of Dr Gillow, has sent out some meritorious and beautiful productions of various classes and orders — statuettes, plaques, vases, flower pots, and so forth. They are, for the most part, painted on by accomplished artists and may be accepted as excellent examples of Art . . . The productions of the Torquay Terra-Cotta Company may be seen at the establishments of Messrs Phillips Brothers in Oxford (Street) and in New Bond Street. They have already obtained much popularity and large sales, and may be safely classed among the most successful issues of Art-manufacture in later times which have come under our notice.'

The outstanding characteristic of this early terracotta was the precision with which it was finished. Indeed, the crispness of both the moulded and turned detail often makes it possible to distinguish a 'Torquay' piece from its Watcombe counterpart by appearance alone. The useful wares were also generally well-proportioned, with restrained decoration. Fig. 42 shows an early example, consisting of a tray fitted with a jug and two beakers, that is marked in pencil as a 'Tap Set' and was intended for draught beer or cider. These articles are moulded in plain terracotta and the vessels glazed internally. Apart from the bands of ribbing they are without any kind of ornamentation, and the severe simplicity of the jug evidently reflects something of the influence of the Arts and Crafts movement.

As far as is known all the domestic terracotta was produced by slip-casting, and the symmetrical hollow-wares finished by turning in treadle-operated lathes. The firm evidently recognized the importance of its turners, because it allowed them to apply their personal stamps to the articles that passed through their hands, and in many cases these inconspicuous little symbols of dots or letters were the only marks applied to the wares. In fact, the quality of the turning was so good that the Torquay Terra-Cotta Company was awarded a medal by the Turners Company, and in 1878 it also obtained an Honourable Mention for its display at the Paris International Exhibition.

Figures and Busts

If the number of statuettes and busts to be found today is any guide, such articles must have formed a larger proportion of the output at Hele Cross than at Watcombe. Amongst the figures produced by the Torquay Terra-Cotta Company works by well-known nineteenth century sculptors are said to have been popular and Brian Reade mentions, in particular, reproductions of John Gibson's 'Tinted Venus'. In general, though, the subjects of the modelled articles were more varied than the early Watcombe figures and busts, with less emphasis on copies of classical works.

The Torquay Museum has a small, but interesting, collection of articles made at Hele Cross that includes a copy of a contemporary figure of a young girl in tattered clothing asleep on a flight of steps (Fig. 43). This has the moulded title 'HOMELESS', together with the inscription 'Emmeline Halse fecit'. Emmeline Halse was a talented sculptress who exhibited regularly at the Royal Academy during the last quarter of the nineteenth century, and this piece was evidently copied from one of her works. Another 'Torquay' figure in the Museum is of a youthful sculptor in Italian renaissance costume, engaged in chiselling the face of a satyr from a block of 'stone' (Fig. 44). This has no title, but is marked 'Zocchi Sc.' and 'Registered August 24th, 1877'. It is paired by a similar figure of an artist. Unfortunately nothing is known about this modeller, and his name does not appear in the standard reference books.

Following Watcombe practice, the Torquay Terra-Cotta Company seems never to have encouraged its artists to sign their work in full. As mentioned, the better pieces sometimes carry the name of the sculptor or modeller as well as the title; but these names are usually moulded, rather than incised, indicating that they are only copies of original works produced elsewhere. There is a tradition in Torquay that Italian modellers were engaged by the early terracotta firms, but it is not established whether they were employed in creating original work, or whether they were only mould makers and assemblers of parts produced from the moulds.

One point in favour of some local modelling capability is that, although the Hele Cross figures were mainly composed of slip-moulded parts, the fine detail in the faces, hair, hands, and feet can often be seen to have been formed, or accentuated, with a tool. Such hand-work is evident, for example, in the standing figure shown in Fig. 45. This model is one of a pair, and is thought to be based on a figure called 'The Bather' which was exhibited at the Royal Academy in 1881 by J.M. Mohr. Mohr submitted a number of works to the Academy about this time, from various addresses in London and on the Continent. He was also the artist responsible for the terracotta portrait plaque of Mr Brock of the Watcombe Pottery shown in Plate II, so he must have had a fairly close association with the Torquay factories.

The ultimate in fineness of modelling, however, were the firm's small busts, of which the portraits in the Torquay Museum of the Prince and Princess of Wales (later to become King Edward VII and Queen Alexandra) are good examples. From the amount of detail apparent in the photograph of the Prince in Fig. 46 it might be supposed that these are of life size, but they are in fact only four inches high. Although they carry no factory mark it may be assumed that they were made at Hele Cross since they were presented to the Torquay Natural History Society by the Torquay Terra-Cotta Company.

The 'Torquay' factory does not appear to have made much use of washes of lighter or darker clay to emphasize the drapery on modelled figures in the Watcombe manner. Nor were the 'Torquay' figures usually decorated with coloured enamels. On the other hand, the moulded birds produced at Hele Cross seem to have been a speciality of the firm that was never copied by Watcombe. These birds are not often seen, but one example noted consisted of a pair of cockatoos perched on a tree stump, slip-cast in plain terracotta.

Enamel and Unglazed Decoration

It is difficult to generalize about the 'Torquay' decorated wares, principally vases, since so few authenticated examples are available. Even so, several distinctive styles can be distinguished during the thirty years of the firm's existence. During the late 'seventies and early 'eighties the preference was for vases of classical shape, with sharply turned outlines, that were sometimes very much like those produced at Watcombe. The decoration during this period was of a restrained character and often consisted of bands of repeating motifs done in enamels round the neck, body, or foot of the article. An excellent example of this type of ware, enamelled in black and white, is the vase of Fig. 47 in the Torquay Museum. This shape was made in various sizes and also served, with the addition of a handle, as an ornamental ewer. Another early style of decoration involved delicate scroll designs in turquoise and white enamels done on vases of renaissance derivation, while matt black and gold banding is found on many articles. Nevertheless, it seems that the turquoise colour was not used as extensively at Hele Cross as at Watcombe.

An entirely different kind of decoration applied to classical vases is typified by the example illustrated in Fig. 48. This has a band of light-coloured slip applied round the centre of the body on which two groups of Grecian warriors have been painted in puce. At first sight these figures might be taken for transfer prints, and only a magnifying glass reveals that they were drawn with a fine 'pencil' brush. Although unsigned, there can be no doubt that this decoration was the work of Alexander Fisher senior, who was one of the two important painters associated with the Torquay Terra-Cotta Company.

Alexander Fisher is said to have come to Torquay from Stoke-on-Trent, and specialized in mythological subjects and flower compositions — an unusual combination. In his spare time, and after his retirement, he taught painting and did water colours for sale. One of his paintings, of roses, is now in the Victoria and Albert Museum and other examples appear occasionally in the sale-rooms. His son, also named Alexander, worked at Hele Cross for a time and after the closure of the terracotta works became a noted designer of Art Nouveau metalwork.

By 1882 the firm had evidently introduced additional types of decoration on its ornamental wares, for it was advertising in the *Pottery Gazette* as:

'THE TORQUAY TERRA-COTTA CO. LTD.

Hele Cross, Torquay.

Manufacturers of Terra-Cotta & Fine Art Pottery.

Decorations in the highest style of Art, in Barbotine,* Underglaze, and Enamel. Plain terra-cotta for amateur painting.'

This indicates that it was already moving away from the more severe classical and renaissance styles to the less formal types of decoration favoured by the contemporary Art movement. In fact, the distinction between the plain terracotta and the 'Fine Art Pottery' lay mainly in the adoption of naturalistic painting on the decorated wares, both in enamels and underglaze work, in place of the earlier stylized motifs. In the early 'eighties this free style of enamel decoration often consisted of extended sprays of foliage and flowers painted round an urn-shaped vase as if actually climbing up it (Plate IV). Later in the decade the enamel tended to cover more of the surface of an article, such as a complete panel of a flask, with the terracotta left exposed only as a surround.

Another example of informal enamel decoration is provided by the jug shown in Fig. 49, painted with a bird and water plants. This subject is found on various articles, sometimes with an enamelled background and sometimes, as in this case, painted direct onto the terracotta. Its particular interest, however, lies in the fact that it is obviously a precursor of the popular 'Kingfisher' design which reached its final form at the Watcombe and Longpark potteries in the 1920s.

The Torquay Terra-Cotta Company is not usually associated with topographic decoration, but the plaque shown in Fig. 50 appears to anticipate the landscapes that were painted underglaze at the Watcombe and Longpark potteries in Edwardian times. This curiously attractive article, which was probably done in the early 'eighties, is decorated with a view of Kenilworth castle — further evidence of the popularity

---

*'Barbotine' was the description generally applied by the Torquay potteries to unglazed slip or modelled clay decoration.

of Scott's novels with the customers of the Torquay potteries. The medium used was a matt black pigment applied directly to the terracotta, with touches of white enamel for the highlights, creating an overall effect like that of a crayon drawing. Since the decoration is fired-on and the rim provided with a matt gold border, this plaque cannot be the work of an amateur and must have been painted in the factory. But the only clue to the identity of the artist is the letter 'W' painted in black on the reverse.

The reference in the advertisement of 1882 to 'plain terra-cotta for amateur painting' shows that the firm also made and sold undecorated blanks to meet the contemporary fashion amongst young ladies for painting in oils on terracotta plaques instead of canvas. It is, perhaps, significant that the advertisement did not claim that the Torquay Terra-Cotta Company sold articles that had been so decorated in the factory. Indeed, since most of the pieces of oil-painted terracotta encountered today are found to be impressed with the Watcombe stamp, this class of ware must have formed only a small proportion of the output of the 'Torquay' Works, if it was done at all.

Underglaze Decoration

Enamel decoration, with the ever-present risk of contamination of the adjacent terracotta surface, must have been a very difficult process to work, and during the late 'eighties it seems to have been discontinued in favour of conventional underglaze painting. This latter type of decoration, usually done on a white ground over the terracotta body, enabled the firm to satisfy the late Victorian taste for colourful ornaments, and the better examples can only be described as magnificent.

Fig. 51 shows one of a pair of vases attributed to Holland Birbeck when he was working at the 'Torquay' factory, probably in the early 'nineties. These are painted underglaze with parrots, in brilliant colours on a pale yellow ground, and finished with gilt outlines and rims. The decoration completely covers the outer surface and only the base and interior disclose the fine red body. In fact, these vases might well be mistaken at a distance for the white clay products of one of the better Staffordshire potteries. This is not surprising, for Holland Birbeck,* who also spent some time at the Watcombe Pottery, came from a family of china decorators whose members worked for various Staffordshire firms during the nineteenth century. Elaborate underglaze decoration in a similar style, but usually involving flowers, was also done at Hele Cross by the elder Alexander Fisher.

Apart from the individually painted vases of Holland Birbeck and the Fishers, which could never have been produced in any great numbers, the Torquay Terra-Cotta Company made several other, simpler, types of decorated and glazed pottery in the last decade of the nineteenth century. In particular, it advertised what was described as 'Crown Devon Ware'.** Although no catalogue illustrations of this type of pottery have been seen, there is reason to believe that it consisted of a range of both useful and ornamental articles decorated under a clear glaze with sprays of apple blossom in pink and white, with black branches, on a dark green ground. It is also a feature of the decoration that the flowers are done in thick pigment to give an impasto effect. The broad band of ground colour usually occupies only the body of the article; the neck, foot, and handle (if any) being left in glazed terracotta. A typical vase of this kind is illustrated in Fig. 52, and it will be seen that the piece has the neat turned finish characteristic of all 'Torquay' work. Cups, saucers, mugs, and jugs of this sort, in addition to vases, are still fairly common in the Torquay district; sometimes with a black, instead of green, ground. Unfortunately, marked examples are rare.

Later Glazed Wares

During the late 1880s the demand for unglazed terracotta had diminished considerably, and in the last decade of the

---

*It is believed that Holland Birbeck, who also painted water-colours privately, signed this type of work: 'A. Birbeck', his middle name being Alexander.
**'Crown Devon' was a description also used by Fielding's of Stoke-on-Trent to describe some of their twentieth-century wares; but these are unlikely to be confused with any Torquay pottery.

century the Torquay Terra-Cotta Company was producing a range of both useful and ornamental glazed earthenwares. These still employed the original terracotta clay, but were finished with a variety of decorative treatments. Besides the Crown Devon Ware, a particularly effective type of pottery was that finished in flown coloured glazes and known as 'Stapleton Ware', presumably after the place of that name from which veined marble was obtained. This kind of decoration had been pioneered by Henry Tooth at the Linthorpe Pottery near Middlesbrough in the early 'eighties, and is not usually associated with the South Devon potteries. Its introduction at Torquay could either have been prompted by a desire to emulate the Yorkshire firm, or Dr Gillow could have engaged workers from Linthorpe when that Pottery closed down about 1890. Whatever the derivation, the Hele Cross Works mastered the technique of this type of glaze so well that it would be difficult to distinguish unmarked specimens from genuine Linthorpe pottery if it were not that the Linthorpe body is usually a toffee-brown colour, without the red tinge of the Torquay clay.

Stapleton Ware was made in various colours, ranging from dark purple to soft greens and blues, often with white speckling that looks like curdled milk. Fig. 53 shows a large vase of Oriental shape decorated in this way with flown green and grey glazes incorporating the typical white flocculations. The base of this piece carries the impressed monogram of the Torquay Terra-Cotta Company and the body has been turned to a smooth surface that accentuates the richness of the glaze. Bottle vases and shallow bowls have also been seen decorated in this way. Although some examples are un-marked, the word 'STAPLETON' is occasionally found impressed in addition to, or instead of, one of the recognized factory marks.

It does not appear that flown glaze effects were produced at Hele Cross for very long — at the most between 1885 and 1905, and possibly only during the 'nineties. This type of ware is therefore comparatively scarce, although the technique was copied by other Torquay potteries, usually with inferior results, until as late as the 1920s.

The Turn of the Century

By the end of the nineteenth century the Torquay Terra-Cotta Company seems to have lost its original impetus and was showing signs of stagnation. The firm never succeeded in establishing a large overseas market like the Watcombe Pottery, nor did it attempt to introduce 'popular' type glazed earthenwares. Eventually, the Works were closed down early in the present century and the moveable effects sold off. The date of the closure is given by some authorities as 1909 but, as will be seen, this cannot be correct since a new firm had acquired the premises by 1908. The last mention of the Torquay Terra-Cotta Company in Kelly's Directory occurs in the 1904 edition and the original firm probably ceased production about 1905, although it is possible that it was not officially 'wound up' until some years later.

Incidentally, there is a sequel to these events which shows how easy it is for misleading legends to become established. When the contents of the first Hele Cross Pottery were sold the 'place boards', on which the ware was moved from one part of the works to another, were bought by the Watcombe Pottery. As a result of seeing these boards in daily use, all branded with the words 'Torquay Terra-Cotta Co.', the belief arose among the Watcombe workmen that this was the original name of their own firm — a belief that is still firmly held to this day by some of the old potters of St. Marychurch!

When the Torquay Terra-Cotta Works closed it had been in existence for barely thirty years, and was a much smaller concern than the Watcombe Pottery. Nevertheless, it had maintained a consistently high standard and never descended to the trivial or over-sentimental of which Watcombe was capable even in the nineteenth century. Examples of the wares of the first Hele Cross Pottery are now scarce, but it is fair to say that they represent some of the finest terracotta ever made in Torquay — perhaps, even, in the whole of the country.

3.2 THE TORQUAY POTTERY

Where lies the land to which the ship would go?
Far, far ahead, is all her seamen know.
And where the land she travels from? Away,
Far, far behind, is all that they can say.

A.H. Clough: Songs in Absence.

After the demise of the Torquay Terra-Cotta Company the Hele Cross Works remained unoccupied for several years. Then, about 1908, the premises were acquired by a Mr Enoch ('Nockie') Staddon, who had previously worked at the Bovey Pottery and whose family originally hailed from Bristol. One of Mr Staddon's first actions was to engage a yard boy to clear the overgrown drive and give access to the Works. He then set about modernizing the Pottery by installing belt-driven throwing wheels, and other machinery, in the single-storey building where the old terracotta had once been cast and turned. Even so, the work-rooms were never comfortable by present standards, for when it rained the water came down the hillside and under the doors and the occupants had to put down boards to walk on. In the course of time Mr Staddon also replaced the original bottle-kiln with two larger ones, and refurbished the box kiln retained from the earlier business.

Pre-War Wares

The original name of the new firm was 'The Torquay Pottery', with the emphasis on Pottery as distinct from Terra-Cotta. However, it continued to be known locally as the 'Hele Cross Pottery' and some early wares were actually stamped with this name. Mr Staddon was evidently a man with ambitions very different to those of Dr Gillow. His intention seems to have been, quite simply, to make red-bodied pottery at prices that would enable him to compete with the existing Torquay factories. Although initially the firm produced some simple articles, such as plaques, in unglazed terracotta (Fig. 54), the bulk of its output consisted of glazed popular wares of the kind already being made at Watcombe and Longpark.

The processes employed at Hele Cross included moulding, slip-casting, turning and jolleying; although most of the ornamental wares were hand-thrown. One of the large kilns was used for pottery in saggars and the other for 'shelf work', with the articles standing on stilts. In order to reduce costs to a minimum, biscuit and glazed wares were fired simultaneously in one kiln so that, as it was said, 'the gloss paid for the biscuit'.

In the five or six years before the start of the Great War, Mr Staddon gathered together a team of about twenty men and boys to carry on the business of the Pottery. It is fortunate that a group photograph of this period has been preserved, albeit much faded, by an old potter who can still identify most of his colleagues of sixty years ago. This photograph (Fig. 56) is a most interesting record, for it represents a virtual microcosm of the Torquay pottery industry of about 1915. Not only does it include two of the best-known decorators — Harry Birbeck* and Harry Crute, who must both have come from Watcombe — but the descriptions of their various jobs show how specialized were the activities of the employees of even a comparatively small pottery at that time.

The photograph is also useful in establishing the types of pottery then being made at Hele Cross. No doubt the articles standing out on the grass, bedecked with bunches of wild flowers for the occasion, represent the best examples of the

*Henry Birbeck, always known as Harry, was the son of Holland Birbeck.

latest styles — chiefly tall, slightly tapered, vases that faintly echo the fashionable Art Nouveau shapes of the previous decade. All of them seem to be made of red clay, and many have dimpled sides and wavy rims. In addition, there are a few globular-bodied jugs of traditional country shape, while the turner displays his skill with a set of covered jars or, possibly, teapots. It is interesting to see that the vases are decorated with continuous 'views' depicting either rustic scenes of cottages and windmills, or fishing boats, of the kind just introduced at Watcombe. As at the larger firm, the Hele Cross panoramas were done in faience-type underglaze painting, using pigment colours applied over a white or cream ground produced by first dipping the article in thin slip. Although windmills are not often seen, the fishing boats were very popular and continued to be produced until at least the late 'twenties. As can be seen from Fig. 55 these were simply, but effectively, drawn. They were also luridly coloured; the ships being painted in black on a blue-green sea, with a bright rose-coloured band above the horizon to represent a sunset. In addition, most articles had the name of the seaside resort, at which they were intended to be sold, painted or scratched on their sides, often with a motto as well for good measure.

Roses and Birds

Apart from scenic decoration, the Torquay Pottery produced the usual range of predominantly cream-and-green coloured slip-wares in the years before the Great War. These incuded vases, jardinieres and pedestals with scratched mottoes and Scandy-type decoration. It does not, however, seem to have evolved any characteristic patterns of its own at this time. During and just after the War, though, the firm introduced several new styles of decoration which, even if they did not all originate at Hele Cross, are more typical of the Torquay Pottery than of any of the other factories. Like the views, many of these were painted underglaze on a cream ground. This was a time when roses were a fashionable decorative motif, and Fig. 57 shows part of a tea-service painted with red 'cabbage' roses on a ground that shades from cream to green, an effect obtained by the use of an air brush. Although the general appearance of this pattern is reminiscent of the roses associated with the Scottish 'Wemyss Ware' it was more probably copied from the Longpark Pottery, which had introduced a similar design just before the War.

Another, slightly later, Hele Cross pattern involving roses, this time of the 'Alexandra' or wild variety, is represented by the dressing-table set of Fig. 58. This is decorated with stylized pink and white flowers with green leaves, outlined in black against a streaky, dark pink, background. The object resembling a large pepper-pot is a hatpin-holder — a characteristic product of the Torquay potteries during the first quarter of the present century. The black borders are typical of the early 'twenties, and the scratched motto seems to have been provided as an essential feature of South Devon pottery.

Colourful birds had always been popular with the decorators at the Torquay potteries. It is not surprising, therefore, that peacocks also formed the subject of painted decoration at Hele Cross, even though in the 'twenties they had long ceased to be a fashionable motif in the Art world. A typical example is the rather sombre vase, shown in Fig. 59, on which the bird has been formed in low relief and then painted in colours against a cream ground that shades to black over the rest of the body. Another, more cheerful, design involving a bird was that done by most of the potteries of the Torquay district, and known as the 'Kingfisher' pattern. This was usually painted on a blue ground and small pieces of Hele Cross ware, often of poor quality and dating to the late 'twenties or 'thirties, can be found decorated in this way. But in the early 'twenties the firm produced much better quality examples done on a creamy yellow ground, and a jardiniere decorated in this way is shown in Fig. 60.

One of the difficulties in writing about Mr Staddon's Pottery is to find a short and unambiguous name for the firm. According to the Trade Directories, the registered name throughout most of its existence was 'The Torquay Pottery Company Limited', although during its later years it seems to have been reconstituted as 'The Torquay Pottery Co. (1932) Ltd'. Nevertheless, to refer to it simply as the 'Torquay Pottery' can, in some contexts, imply a reference to the whole of the local industry. Perhaps the firm felt the same difficulty, for it used a variety of marks on its wares at different times. As mentioned, some articles made before the mid-'twenties bear the words 'Hele Cross Pottery' impressed or painted. The usual mark in the early 'twenties, however, was 'Torquay/Pottery/England', incised, although combinations and variants of these two marks are also encountered. Unfortunately, the scratched marks are very faint and all but obliterated by the thick glaze which usually covers the flat base of an article; while many pieces seem never to have been marked at all.

In the absence of a decipherable mark it is worth noting that articles made at the Torquay Pottery usually had a very fine light red body, comparable to the best Watcombe. This is not surprising, since the clay came from the same pit that had been used by the earlier Torquay Terra-Cotta Company for their unglazed wares. But even the Hele Cross clay eventually deteriorated in quality and late pieces often have a dark brown body, more like some Longpark. From the early 'twenties, however, identification was made much easier by the general adoption of a rubber-stamped mark. For a short time the wording was still 'TORQUAY/POTTERY/ENGLAND', in block capitals, but after Mr Staddon had sold a pair of vases to Queen Mary at the Empire Exhibition at Wembley in 1924 the firm adopted the style 'Royal Torquay Pottery' and the mark was changed accordingly. Incidentally, the Torquay Pottery was the only one of the larger firms in the district that did not normally mark its wares with pattern numbers, either for shape or for decoration.

Moulded Wares

All the vases described so far appear to have been thrown on the wheel. However, the Torquay Pottery was unusual in that it continued to produce articles that were wholly or partly moulded, at a time when most other potteries in the district had virtually abandoned this method of production. One relatively simple style of decoration adopted before the Great War involved moulded butterflies attached to various articles. Fig. 61 shows a candlestick treated in this way; the butterfly

G

being painted underglaze and appearing to hover over a clump of painted bulrushes. In order, presumably, to reduce the risk of damage, these butterflies are very thickly and crudely moulded, reminding one of Tenniel's illustration of the 'bread-and-butter flies' in *Alice in Wonderland*. Even so, they must have been quite vulnerable, and undamaged examples are now hard to find.

The other article shown in Fig. 61 is a candle snuffer, in the form of a peacock standing on a tree-stump, which seems to have been moulded from plastic clay rather than slip-cast. Unfortunately for this model Mr Staddon was a superstitious man and when, during a spell of bad trade, it was suggested to him that peacocks were unlucky, he went into the factory and smashed all the moulds. After this incident peacocks were never again allowed to appear on Hele Cross wares!

Some moulded or slip-cast articles produced by the Torquay Pottery were quite elaborate. This was a time when electricity was being brought to the country districts of South Devon (and elsewhere, of course) and there was a growing demand for ornamental light fittings. Mr Staddon therefore took the opportunity of introducing decorative earthenware table lamp bases, including one in the form of an owl (Fig. 62) and another of a parrot on its perch. Although the owl sold well, very few copies of the parrot were made because the modeller gave the bird three claws at the front of each foot and one at the back, instead of two at the front and two at the back. Eventually the mistake was pointed out to Mr Staddon, and then this mould suffered the same fate as that of the peacock!

Toby jugs are not the kind of article usually associated with the Torquay potteries, yet both the Watcombe and Hele Cross works made them in the period between the Wars. The only available photograph of the interior of the Hele Cross Works (Fig. 63) does, by chance, show a batch of these articles at the dipping stage. They were mostly quite small, slip-cast, and decorated underglaze in red and blue over the white ground. From Toby jugs it was, perhaps, only natural that the firm should progress to other types of slip-cast face jugs, and at one time Mr Staddon introduced a series of jugs moulded and painted to represent the eight characters in the ballad of *Widecombe Fair* (Fig. 64). These were modelled by Mr Staddon's brother-in-law, Mr Vincent Kane (Fig. 56), and held about a quart. Each one had the appropriate name scratched through the slip round the collar, e.g.: 'Dan'l Widdon from Widecombe Fair', and at a distance they appear to be made of thin white china, rather than red earthenware. Unfortunately only a few sets were ever made owing, it is understood, to the cost of packing such large and fragile articles.

In the early 'twenties the Widecombe Fair ballad also provided the subject for a range of mugs and other articles decorated in low relief with Tom Pearce's grey mare and her riders. In the example shown in Fig. 65(a) the figures appear to have been moulded separately, sprigged on to the body of the piece and then picked out in bright colours. The opposite side of the mug carries the names of the characters involved, done in sgraffito. A similar type of decoration occurs on the 'Clovelly' jug illustrated in Fig. 65(b). Here the central part of the view of the village is an applied low-relief moulding, but the painting continues the perspective over the surrounding surface of the jug.

Blue Grounds

In the mid-'twenties there was a marked change in the colour schemes used by the Torquay Pottery, with a dark, bright, blue replacing green and cream as the usual ground colour. During the same period scenic painting was gradually discontinued and decorative designs became simpler and more stylized. The fashion for blue grounds was, of course, not confined to Hele Cross, for this colour was generally adopted by Watcombe and Longpark at about the same time, and is characteristic of most Torquay-made pottery of the 'thirties. This change seems to have coincided with the introduction of women as decorators, an innovation that was probably intended to off-set rising production costs after the War.

Although not an 'important' piece in collecting terms, the small vase shown in Fig. 66 is helpful in establishing an approximate epoch for this transition. It is, unusually, signed and dated: 'F. Bowden, Jan. 17, 1923', and exhibits both early and late features; having a carefully painted scene of a cottage by a stream, but done on a blue ground. Slip-painted cottages on a cream ground were never very popular at the Torquay Pottery, although articles are occasionally found decorated with rustic buildings of various shapes in imitation of Watcombe's Cottage Ware.

The most typical, and probably the earliest, of the standard blue-ground patterns at Hele Cross was the parrot design (Fig. 67). This usually shows a parrot, in low relief and garishly painted in bright colours, perched on a black, painted, tree with sponged green and yellow foliage; all done on a bright blue ground over the red body, and highly glazed. As with the contemporary Widecombe Fair mugs, these parrots were separately moulded and then applied to the thrown body, although the joint is difficult to detect under the coatings of slip and glaze. After being in production for several years, the Parrot design was simplified by the omission of all but the most rudimentary details of tree and foliage. Perhaps as compensation, it then became the custom to apply two parrots (possibly 'love birds') sitting side by side. In the early 'twenties the streaky mauve-pink ground was occasionally used instead of dark blue, while on some articles the birds were pheasants or owls. Yet, despite the apparent popularity of this style of decoration, it was never copied by any of the other potteries in Torquay.

Other blue-ground patterns of the Torquay Pottery in the 'twenties included the rosette design represented by the vase of Fig. 68, and various slip and pigment-decorated flowers and butterflies. The first-mentioned is thickly painted with orange and green leaves over a mottled blue ground produced by spongeing blue slip over a white undercoat. The butterfly pattern shown in the same photograph is obviously a simplification of the earlier moulded version. It should be noted, though, that several styles of decoration done at Hele Cross during this period were also produced at Mr Staddon's other firm: the Bovey Tracey Art Pottery (see Sect. 7). For example, the bowl on the left of Fig. 68, which was made at Bovey, has the same shape as the butterfly bowl but the decoration of the tall vase.

These blue-ground wares were not usually provided with mottoes, presumably because of the lack of contrast between the colours of the ground and the body. This is illustrated by the shallow candlestick of Fig. 67, where the inscription is difficult to read even on the actual article.

Yet another Royal Torquay pattern, probably dating to the early 'thirties, appears on the jug of Fig. 70. This distinctive shape, which seems to have been confined to Hele Cross, is finished in this example in a uniform blue colour with a band of oval motifs (possibly stylized leaves) done in pigment colours over a white ground at the neck. Not all Royal Torquay pottery, however, had a blue ground, and Fig. 69 shows a tall covered vase of distinguished and Oriental shape that is decorated in the manner of early faience with broad, restrained, brush strokes done in thin pigment colours on a white ground.

The 'Thirties

The depression years of the nineteen-thirties saw intense competition between the Torquay potteries to retain their individual shares of the market for souvenir wares. No new kinds of decoration were introduced at Hele Cross during this period, although faience-type painting on a white ground seems to have enjoyed something of a revival, with various fruits — including apples, grapes, and cherries — as alternatives to flowers. The style of this painting was essentially the same as that done fifteen or twenty years earlier, except that more colourful sprayed borders were used, with violet and yellow sometimes combined on one article.

Mr Staddon, who is said to have had a 'keen business sense', caused a great deal of resentment amongst other firms in the 'thirties by cutting prices. Apart from his existing practice of firing biscuit and gloss together he adopted various other measures intended to reduce production costs. As a result, the general quality of the ware deteriorated, with what was by then a coarse brown body often showing through the skimped coating of ground colour. Most of the articles turned out at this time were small vases, teapots, ash-trays and similar mementoes, and for many years one of the minor staple products had been little conical bottles intended to hold 'Devon Violets' scent (Fig. 71). As one of his economies Mr Staddon decided to omit the internal coat of glaze on a batch of these, with the result that, as the story is still told: 'the scent ran out of the front door as soon as it was poured into the bottles'. But by this time the firm was more concerned with keeping its head above water than maintaining its reputation, and adopted the practice of selling its wares by the kiln-full to the local branch of a chain-store.

Even if hostilities had not commenced in 1939, it is doubtful whether the Torquay Pottery could have survived for much longer by these methods. As it was, the firm found itself obliged to close down early in the Second World War by the restrictions imposed on the production of decorated wares. Mr Staddon then retired to the village of Compton, just outside Torquay, and at the end of the War set up another small Pottery at his home, using an electric kiln and selling to visitors.

With the return of peace the larger part of what had been the Hele Cross Pottery was converted into a laundry. The workshops and kilns, however, remained derelict until the mid-'sixties, when they were demolished and replaced by ovens of a different kind — for baking meat pies! Nevertheless, the determined visitor can still walk up the drive from Barton Hill Road and see the terracotta 'enrichments' on the old Pottery building that bear the proud initials 'T.T.C.' and the date '1876'.

TORQUAY TERRA-COTTA COMPANY MARKS

(i) *Factory Marks.* Some articles of 'Torquay' manufacture were not given a factory mark, while others will be found bearing both impressed and transfer-printed marks.

18. **TORQUAY** Impressed mark. 1875 – c.1905.

19.   Printed or impressed mark. 1875 – c.1905.

20.  Printed or impressed mark, 1875 – c.1890.

21.  Printed or impressed mark. 1875 – c.1890.

22.   Printed or Impressed mark c.1895 — c.1905.

23.   **STAPLETON**   Impressed mark, usually found on articles finished with flown glazes. c.1890 — c.1905.

(ii) *Turners' Marks*. Most 'Torquay' terracotta with a turned finish was impressed by the turner with his personal stamp. It should be noted, however, that No. 24(a) is also found on Watcombe terracotta, and is possibly the mark of a Mr Willott.

24 (a) ⩔ (b) ▪▪▪ (c) W

(iii) *Pattern Numbers*. Terracotta articles sometimes have a number, of up to three digits, painted on the base in small black letters. These are believed to refer to the style of decoration.

(iv) *Modellers' and Decorators' Marks*. Most 'Torquay' ware is unsigned. The incised or moulded 'signatures' found on terracotta figures and busts appear to refer to the original sculptor or modeller from whose work the article was copied. The senior decorators at Hele Cross were Alexander Fisher senior (flowers and classical figure subjects), Alexander Fisher junior, and Holland Birbeck (flowers and birds), who also worked at Watcombe. One plaque decorated in pigment and enamels has been noted with the painted initial 'W' on the back.

TORQUAY POTTERY COMPANY MARKS

(i) *Factory Marks*. Most articles appear to have been marked, although the scratched marks used before about 1923 can easily pass unnoticed.

25. HELE CROSS TORQUAY POTTERY

    Impressed mark on early terra-cotta. 1908—c.1915.

26. TORQUAY POTTERY ENGLAND

    Rare impressed mark: 1908—c.1930.

27. TORQUAY POTTERY

    Painted mark on pigment-decorated articles. c.1910—1924.

28. Torquay Pottery Torquay England

    Scratched mark commonly found on glazed articles, c.1910—1924. Usually only partly decipherable.

29 (a). *Hele Cross Pottery Torquay, England*

Various painted marks, incorporating the words 'Hele Cross' or 'Torquay Pottery' or both, found on pigment-decorated wares made c.1910—1920.

(b). *Torquay Pottery Co Hele Cross Torquay Devon*

30.	HELE CROSS POTTERY TORQUAY	Rare rubber-stamped mark. c.1912—1918.
31.	TORQUAY POTTERY ENGLAND	Rubber-stamped mark. c.1918—1924.
32.	ROYAL TORQUAY POTTERY ENGLAND	The usual late mark, rubber-stamped: 1924—1940.

(ii) *Pattern Numbers.* Early slip-wares decorated with the 'Scandy' pattern were sometimes incised with 'N.1', but later pigment-decorated articles seldom have anything but the factory mark.

(iii) *Artists' Marks.* Although Henry ('Harry') Birbeck and Harry Crute both worked at Hele Cross about the time of the Great War no articles signed or initialled by either of these decorators have been encountered. Only one signed article has been seen: a vase with 'F. Bowden' and a date in 1923 painted on the base.

Section Four

ALLER VALE

Fig. iii.   Mr John Phillips, proprietor of the Aller Vale Pottery. From a photograph probably taken just before his death in 1897.

Here's Coffinswell and Kings Kerswell!
And here's for Abbots Kerswell too!
'Tis where we merry craftsmen dwell,
And wondrous is the work we do!

Refrain of *Song of the 'Three Wells'*
by 'E.P.'

During the third quarter of the nineteenth century a small
pottery Works was operating in the hamlet of Aller, half-way
between Kings Kerswell and Newton Abbot and just off the
main road to Torquay. In those days the place consisted of
little more than a farmhouse, a few cottages, and a mill on the
Aller brook, which runs along the bottom of the wide valley.
The business had been established in 1865 to make ordinary
domestic pots and pans, but after only three years it was
acquired by a Mr John Phillips, who then lived at Newton
Abbot. Mr Phillips reorganized the pottery to concentrate on
the production of builders' earthenware, and in the 1870
edition of Morris's Directory of Devonshire the firm is listed as
'Phillips, John & Co., manufacturers of architectural pottery
and firebricks'. According to Llewellynn Jewitt the goods
produced at this time consisted mainly of roofing tiles, pipes,
and garden edgings, together with ornamental chimney pots
and bricks. Nevertheless, some simple domestic wares,
including flower vases, continued to be made and this enabled

the firm to claim in later years, with some justification, that it was the oldest-established of all the Torquay potteries.

In his novel *Brunel's Tower* Eden Phillpotts makes his chief character, a master potter from Staffordshire, break his journey to Torquay in the 1880s at what is obviously the Aller Pottery. Here he finds:

'a cluster of low buildings surmounted by familiar cones. Here spread a potter's field and stood pottery works in a little vale. Green fields rolled about; above them towered the edges of a wood, while beyond the buildings a stream ran where spread water-meadows bright with king-cups.'

After this idyllic description of the Pottery's surroundings it comes as a surprise when the novelist continues by saying that the workmen:

'showed a heavy indifference to fortune and an extreme lack of interest in their toil, . . . it seemed that their brains were turned to clay by their work.'

However, these remarks are so much at variance with the facts that they must be regarded just as artistic licence, intended to establish the superiority of the Longpark Pottery which forms the main setting of Phillpotts' story.

Cottage Art Schools

In the year 1879 a small Art School was formed in the village of Kings Kerswell on the initiative of a local Physician, Dr Symonds. According to the Rev Baring Gould, this institution was originally associated with the village Sunday-school and began by teaching drawing to local farm workers in what little spare time they had in those days. The classes were started in the kitchen of a cottage occupied by a widow, Mrs Mary Bulley, and were financed by fortnightly 'entertainments' given by the students, rather than by fees. The school was later extended to the cottage next door, where another room was made available for carpentry lessons. The success of this venture led to the formation of similar schools in the neighbouring villages of Abbots Kerswell and Coffinswell, with a total attendance of over sixty pupils. Eventually, the three schools were combined in order to support a qualified art instructor.

Although Dr Symonds did not live to see more than the beginning of these classes, Mr Phillips was also a patron of the original school and in the year that it was founded he moved to a house called Moor Park, close to the Pottery on the sloping ground between the main road and the stream. In fact, Mr Phillips may well have been the real driving force behind the scheme. As a prominent member of the Devonshire Association he had campaigned for many years for the establishment of what he called Cottage Art Schools. He also gave many lectures on Arts and Crafts training, including one entitled 'The Potter's Art in Devonshire'. Apart from this, he was well known as a local historian and antiquarian and had encouraged a North Devon potter (George Fishley of Fremington) to copy specimens of antique pottery in the British Museum. It is not surprising, therefore, that after a serious fire at the Aller Works in 1881 he decided to rebuild with the intention of making Art pottery, particularly terracotta. In taking this step he was no doubt, influenced by the success of the new terracotta factories at Torquay, and by the availability of suitable employees from amongst the pupils of the local Art Schools.

According to a near-contemporary account, Mr Phillips's original object was 'philanthropical rather than commercial, (being) to find useful and elevating employment for the leisure of boys and youths of country villages, and to raise the taste of the cottagers by replacing their ornaments and utensils with others of a type superior in design, but not expensive or superfine.' To this end, when the Pottery had been rebuilt, Mr Phillips engaged some of the more adept students, who were given instruction in throwing by an experienced potter. (The latter is said to have been a 'gipsy', but this term probably implied simply an itinerant craftsman.)

When the Aller Works were reopened the Watcombe Pottery had been in operation for ten years, and was at the height of its popularity, while the rival Torquay Terra-Cotta Company had been established for about half that time. Both these firms had acquired reputations for high-quality terracotta of classical derivation but Mr Phillips evidently decided to avoid this style, which was, in any case, going out of fashion in the early 'eighties. He provided his trainees, instead, with examples of 'Egyptian, Persian, Italian, French, Japanese and even English' pottery to copy, 'which are enough to frighten away all the native art spirits which haunt the ferny lanes of Devonshire', as Cosmo Monkhouse cynically observed in the *Magazine of Art*. For his terracotta wares Mr Phillips also turned to various unconventional and often exotic styles of the kind favoured by the contemporary Art movement. At the same time, presumably to suit more conservative customers, he introduced a range of articles based mainly on traditional West Country shapes and methods of decoration.

Early Art Wares

The early Aller terracotta Art wares seem to have been formed mainly by slip-casting; except for plaques, which were probably made from plastic clay and turned to shape. Examples are now very rare, but the Exeter Museum has several articles of this period bearing the incised marks: 'Phillips/Aller' or 'Phillips/Newton Abbot'. These are all moulded, but they have an irregularity of form and finish that immediately distinguishes them from the more sophisticated Watcombe terracotta, which was produced by experienced modellers and mould-makers from Staffordshire. Fig. 72 shows one of these pieces, a vase with an onion-shaped body and long neck. Earthenware bottles were popular at the time with other Art potteries, but instead of a conventional foot-ring this vase has a crimped clay strip attached to its base (possibly intended as a deliberately 'rustic' feature) to enable it to stand upright.

Other examples of early Aller terracotta consist of strangely shaped moulded jugs and handled bottles (Fig. 73). These are provided with low-relief decoration in the manner of some pre-Columbian American pottery, possibly in imitation of some of the wares then being made by the Linthorpe Pottery near Middlesbrough. Cosmo Monkhouse's article is illustrated with several further, and little-known, types of Aller pottery, including 'Barbotine' (modelled clay decoration), 'Delft', and 'Majolica'. However, such styles evidently did not appeal to a wide market, and it is not surprising that most of them were soon discontinued.

After two or three years Mr Phillips evidently decided that

the time was ripe to publicize his wares on a national scale, and the firm's first advertisement in the *Pottery Gazette*, which appeared in July 1884, is worth quoting in full for the information it gives:

'DEVONSHIRE FAIENCE & ALLER VALE
TERRA-COTTA
Newton Abbot, Devon.

Faience: Vases, Ewers, etc; in bright glazes, with seaweed, shell, flower and sgraffito decoration. Also in "Amber" and "Huacco Marble".

Terra-Cotta: Thrown and turned plaques, vases, pilgrim bottles in red & buff, also in black lacquer.

Domestic Art Pottery: Pitchers, Aller stoneware jugs, Toby shaped jugs, etc.

The Red and Buff terra-cotta earths, also the clays for the faience are raised on the Works. London agents: Gent & Abbott, Holborn Circus.'

It is interesting to see from this advertisement that Faience, i.e. glazed pottery, had already taken priority over terracotta as the most important class of ware, and that the firm distinguished between the highly-glazed decorated pottery and the ordinary domestic earthenware. According to the generally accepted definition, faience is pottery decorated by painting directly on to a ground of white tin oxide and then glazed. In Victorian times, however, the word 'faience' meant different things to different potteries, and the Devonshire Faience of the Aller Pottery consisted of earthenware decorated underglaze with designs done in coloured slips. The ware was produced by throwing on string-driven wheels (Fig. 74) and included jugs with bulbous bodies and pinched lips, pitchers of barrel shape, mugs and tankards, together with various ornaments and vases. Usually the articles were made from red clay and then dipped, while still in the 'green' state, into thin white slip. This left them with a white surface, on the outside only, to which the decoration proper could subsequently be applied. Alternatively, ornamental designs or lettering could be scratched through this ground to show up in the dark colour of the body.

Nearly all the operations at the rebuilt Aller Pottery were carried on by human effort, without the aid of steam-driven machinery. The exception was the initial preparation of the clay, which was separated from stones and other debris by being churned with water in spiked drums operated by small water-wheels. The liquid clay was then concentrated by being run down heated 'flukes' to evaporate the excess moisture, and finally wedged before use by the throwers. After the wares had been thrown those which were required to be particularly smooth or accurately formed, such as teapot lids, were turned in treadle-operated lathes worked by boy assistants. According to contemporary accounts there were two biscuit kilns and several glost ovens. At least one of the big kilns was built into the centre of the main Pottery building; but although this arrangement was very convenient for production, it made the place uncomfortably hot in summer.

Devonshire Faience

The first type of slip decoration employed at the Aller Pottery consisted of various simple motifs disposed to suit the shape of the article concerned. One of the most popular motifs was a daisy-like arrangement of eight radiating brush strokes, usually done in pale blue and buff, alternating with a group of four curved strokes in dark green arranged in the form of an X. This became known as the 'Abbots Kerswell' pattern, apparently because it was evolved by a decorator who came from that village, and continued to be used for many years on traditional-type wares. Blank spaces outside the main pattern were sometimes filled in with tadpole-like devices done in dark green or blue, while the rims of jugs and vases were usually finished with borders of the same colours. These borders took the form of sinuous lines with spots on either side (supposed to represent seaweed) or a continuous band with curious double-lobed projections.

From the earliest days of the Aller Art Pottery the

slip-decorated wares were often inscribed with mottoes or verses; usually on one side of the article with the decoration on the other, although this is not mentioned in the 1884 advertisement. Also, the ground colour was not invariably white or cream, and a medium blue-grey was occasionally used as an alternative. Identifiable examples of early Phillips wares are now hard to find, but the jugs illustrated in Figs. 76 and 93 show most of the decorative features mentioned. The former is ascribed to the Aller Pottery on the basis of its dark red body and unglazed base and is believed to have been made about 1885. It is not marked with the name of the Works, but with the impressed words 'MADE IN DEVON', presumably in accordance with Mr Phillips's often expressed conviction that Devonshire products were the best in the kingdom. The jug of Fig. 93 was probably made later in the 'eighties, since it has a light orange-red body and glazed base impressed 'ALLER VALE'. However, it retains several other features of the early traditional wares, such as the characteristic ribbed handle with its ends formed into the shape of a leaf.

Descriptions of the Aller Pottery always emphasized that no 'outside' decorators were employed, and that the patterns were all evolved by the local workmen. While this may have been true of the earliest, rather naïve motifs, the firm did nevertheless, retain the services of an Italian artist (a Signor Marcouti) at one time to advise the decorators on suitable designs. Apart from the Abbots Kerswell pattern, which is said to have been developed under his supervision, Signor Marcouti was responsible for a series of scroll patterns which characterized many of the Aller wares until the end of the nineteenth century. Scroll motifs of renaissance origin were, of course, popular throughout the Victorian period for the decoration of all kinds of domestic furnishings. However, the Aller Vale scroll was regarded by the firm as a proprietary design, even though it does not seem to have been given any particular name* (Figs. 80 and 85).

All these designs were applied by brush to the unfired body

*In our *Victorian Art Pottery*, the scroll design was wrongly described as the 'Abbots Kerswell' pattern, owing to a misunderstanding of a contemporary report.

as slips of fairly thick consistency which, even after glazing, left the pattern slightly raised above the surface of the article. The 'bright glazes' mentioned in the advertisement were bright only in the sense that they were glossy; they were not usually coloured like some translucent glazes used by other contemporary Art potteries. The exception was the 'Amber' ware, which was finished in a deep yellow translucent glaze over a dipped coat of white slip, usually without any further decoration. The 'Huacco Marble' finish also mentioned consisted of streaked or mottled slips of several semi-opaque colours splashed or brushed directly on to the brown body of an article. This kind of decoration is not very common but the small dimpled pot shown in Fig. 77 is typical of the effect, the colours including cream, black and green.

Aller Vale Art Wares

Yet another point of interest about the 1884 advertisement is that although the description 'Aller *Vale*' is used, it is applied not to the firm (which is not mentioned by name) but only to its wares. Evidently this was recognized as an unsatisfactory arrangement, and about 1887 the description 'Aller Vale Art Pottery' was adopted as the business name, although still subsidiary to the formal style of 'John Phillips & Company'.

The pottery made between about 1884 and 1887 may be distinguished from the later Aller wares by having an unglazed base which sometimes bears the mark 'Aller Vale' incised in large script lettering. When flat, the base exhibits horse-shoe shaped lines left by the wire used to cut the article from the potter's wheel. Alternatively, some pieces have a turned, recessed, base with the inside of the foot-ring bevelled. Like the jug of Fig. 76 these transitional wares were generally made of a compact red body with a tinge of blue, very like the type of brick that was so popular with Victorian builders. Another characteristic of Aller pottery of the mid-'eighties is the continuing use of handles of 'double ogee' section.

During this period some very colourful and competently decorated pieces were produced. Indeed, some of them are hardly recognized today as being from the Aller Vale Pottery because they do not conform to the popular impression of the firm's later work. Typical of these wares is the thrown and modelled ornament (it can scarcely be described as a vase) shown in Fig. 78. This consists of a handled vessel with two spouts, one for filling and the other — in the form of a bird's head with coxcomb — for pouring, that is a further example of Mr Phillips's penchant for copying ancient pottery. The decoration consists mainly of a chrysanthemum-like flower in the centre of each side, surrounded by a wreath of foliage, while the spouts are painted with eyes for the bird's 'head' and feathers for its 'tail'. The central motif of the decoration (and, possibly, the shape of the article itself) is copied from pottery which was then believed to have been made in the sixteenth century on the island of Rhodes, but is now known to have come from the region of Isnik in Asia Minor.

Not all Aller Vale pottery of the transitional period was decorated with abstract or stylized floral designs, and one occasionally comes across articles with freehand sgraffito treatment of a more spontaneous kind, such as the small jug of Fig. 79. This, again, has the typical red body, dry base, and ribbed handle, with the incised 'Aller Vale' mark, but the outside has a blue-grey ground through which figures of dancing pixies have been scratched. The figures, and the border motifs, are coloured with tinted slips under a clear glaze, much like some of the decoration then being done in the Brannam Pottery at Barnstaple. Evidently, this style of decoration must have become popular for a time, since later versions have been seen with the pixies moulded in low relief on articles bearing the impressed Aller Vale mark.

From old photographs (Fig. 75) it can be seen that the Devonshire Faience was made in batches and all the articles in one batch were decorated with the same pattern. Slip painting on the raw clay was an art that required an assured touch, for the brush had to be applied in exactly the right place and with just the right amount of colour at the first attempt. No second attempt was possible, for once the slip had been laid on it could not be removed without staining the ground. Even the preparation of the ground required a great deal of experience. If the article was not dry enough, and the ground was applied by dipping, the clay could be so softened that it would collapse under its own weight. Whole batches of pots would then 'go down', as it was termed, overnight, and be completely ruined. On the other hand, if the body had been allowed to dry out too far then the handles and spouts could not be stuck on!

White-Clay and other Wares

It is not generally realized that Aller Vale made a considerable amount of earthenware from white clay, for the firm is usually thought of as a red-clay Pottery. As an example of this kind of ware Fig. 80 shows a small tea-service decorated with coloured scrolls, while a scroll design of stylized foliage was also done in pale blue on a range of white-bodied articles. The latter was known, 'by permission of the Princess of Wales', as the 'Sandringham' pattern, and remained in production for many years. Fig. 81 shows a group of articles decorated in this manner, and it will be seen that the design could vary from a dark blue with sharp outlines to a pale blue with soft edges, according to circumstances.

Despite the lack of commercial success of the early Phillips terracotta, the production of this type of ware was not abandoned completely until quite late in the nineteenth century. The firm's advertisements referred to plaques and vases, presumably of conventional type and decorated, as at Watcombe in the late 'eighties and the 'nineties, with sprays of flowers done in oil paints. But the Aller Pottery does not seem to have had artists capable of such elaborate painting as at Watcombe, and the small moulded ornament in the form of a mandolin, shown in Fig 82 is representative of the firm's later terracotta. This typical Victorian fancy is made from a good-quality body, and compares favourably with the Watcombe violin shown for comparison. Other small terracotta articles were decorated in coloured enamels with the arms of various towns and colleges, possibly with the intention of competing with Goss 'heraldic china'.

Although classed with the firm's terracotta products, the ware described as 'Black Lacquer' was finished all over, except on the base, with a shiny black glaze and then decorated with flowers that were hand-painted in oils. This kind of Aller

Plate V. Large cup and stand, made at the Aller Vale Pottery to commemorate the coronation of King Edward VII and Queen Alexandra in 1902. Decorated with coloured slips, applied mouldings, and sgraffito inscription. Made from buff-coloured clay.

pottery, which appears to have been known locally as 'Black Devon' ware, is not often encountered and is usually unmarked, but a small example is shown in Fig. 77.

Another type of Aller pottery, described in the firm's advertisements but seldom encountered these days, was the stoneware. This was made from the local off-white clay and fired to a higher temperature than the other pottery, so that articles of this kind are noticeably heavier than the usual red- and white-bodied wares. As far as can be discovered by inspection, the Aller stoneware was not saltglazed like the contemporary Doulton Ware but was probably finished with a high-temperature clear glaze of 'Bristol' type.

Most of the Aller stoneware seems to have been in the form of useful domestic articles, such as jugs and pitchers, for which a non-porous body was desirable. Fig. 83 shows a jug decorated with horizontal rows of small motifs, impressed by means of 'runners', which is remarkably like the Doulton stoneware jug shown in Fig. 34 of our *Victorian Art Pottery*. Since the latter was made soon after 1870 it is possible that the Aller version was one of Mr Phillips's earlier productions. Later in the nineteenth century some decorated and ornamental stoneware was produced, and this also bore a strong resemblance to the simpler articles of Doulton Ware then being made at Lambeth. The small vase of Fig. 84, which is probably typical of this type of Aller ware, is decorated with blue scrolls on an unusual speckled brown ground, the scrolls being outlined with deeply incised grooves down to the white body.

Late Victorian Styles

By the late 'eighties Mr Phillips's pottery had acquired a character which eventually became associated not only with Aller Vale but with most of the Torquay firms in the twentieth century. These Aller Vale Art Wares were highly glazed all over, including the base, and were typically decorated with simple, but spirited, standardized designs done in coloured slips over a slip-coated ground, often with sgraffito inscriptions in addition. They were usually, but not invariably, made from a fine quality clay of light red colour, like that of Hele Cross, but the true colour of the body was often deliberately obscured and darkened by brown or orange tinted glazes and can only be seen on chipped surfaces. From this time, also, the usual mark was 'ALLER/VALE' impressed in block capitals. Later, in the 'nineties, the words 'DEVON' or 'DEVON/ENGLAND' were normally added.

In 1889 the Aller Pottery had been fortunate in securing the patronage of Princess Louise, Queen Victoria's sculptress daughter. This led to purchases by other members of the Royal Family, and to the adoption by the firm of the style 'Royal Aller Vale Pottery'. It also resulted in the wares being advertised and sold by Liberty's, the London store famous for its Art furnishings. By this time the Renaissance Scroll motif had become one of the most popular types of decoration. In its original form this consisted of whorls of stylized leaves and flowers painted in blended colours of green, blue, brown, peach, and yellow direct on to a white or red body, but in the 'nineties it was often done on a green or blue ground over a red body. Alternatively, plain white leaf scrolls, without the terminal flower-heads, were painted on a dark blue ground, but this is relatively uncommon. Examples of these scroll patterns are shown in Fig. 85.

Liberty's catalogue for 1892 had a whole page devoted to illustrations of 'Aller Vale Ware', including mugs, jugs, flower pots, ornamental plates, and a curiously shaped 'Persian' ewer. These articles all appear to be decorated on a white ground with stylized floral patterns of the kind shown in Fig. 78, and were stated to reproduce 'with the utmost possible correctness, the effect of Old Rhodian Ware, distinguished for its delicacy of colour and quaintness of decoration'. Apart from the prices, which started at 1/- for a 4-inch vase, it is interesting to note that the catalogue also recommended where each article should be placed in a room for the best effect. The ewer, for example, 13 inches high and at 21/- one of the most expensive items, was recommended for sideboard and over-door decoration.

The flowing lines of the Scroll pattern also formed the basis of various semi-formal treatments of leaves and flowers, such as that on the vase of Fig. 86. Towards the end of the century, however, the preference was for more naturalistic sprays of flowers painted in slip on a dark green ground. This style of decoration, of which the waisted jug of Fig. 88 is a typical example, has a simple dignity that is, regrettably, lacking in many of the products of the later Torquay potteries.

Throughout its existence Aller Vale confined its output to ornamental, domestic, and table-wares. Most of these were of comparatively small size, although vases of up to two feet in height were occasionally produced. Large quantities of what were called 'children's toys' (presumably miniatures) were also turned out, and match strikers were evidently a popular line. Yet the Pottery seems to have made few candlesticks — a characteristic it shared with Watcombe. As far as is known, the firm never made figures or busts like its Torquay neighbours, and many of its decorative wares of the 'nineties affected fashionably 'quaint' shapes. These included waisted jugs and vases, often with wavy rims and skewed handles, and multi-necked flower holders which became so typical of the Torquay potteries that their near-Eastern origin (as the shape for a lamp) has been forgotten. Another deliberately contrived oddity was a jug whose handle passed through a hole in its widely flared rim; but it should be noted that this was subsequently copied at Watcombe and Longpark (Fig. 87).

Aller Vale also made commemorative pieces, especially for the 1897 Jubilee, when jugs and beakers were sold bearing inscriptions in praise of the Queen. A few years later, at the time of the Boer War, came articles with suitably patriotic decoration, such as the low-relief figure of a soldier in brown (khaki) flanked by Union Jacks and the words: 'God bless you, Tommy Atkins' (Fig. 89). One of the firm's most impressive, if not the most artistic, creations of this type is the giant standing cup made to commemorate the coronation of King Edward VII in 1902 (Plate V). This is unusual in that the portrait busts, like the figure of the soldier on the Boer War pieces, have been separately moulded and applied to an otherwise conventional scheme of decoration. It is also unusual in being made of a pale buff clay, as were various smaller mugs and beakers done in a similar style.

Although most of the Aller Vale wares consisted of standard shapes that were thrown on the wheel, sometimes modified by a little hand manipulation, unsymmetrical articles were necessarily made by moulding, pressing, or slip-casting. Some, at least, of these moulded pieces were accorded rather more elaborate decorative treatments than the run-of-the-mill patterns. Typical examples are the wall pocket of Fig. 90 and various shell-shaped plates painted with birds and flowers and inscribed with moral quotations. Yet another type of ware introduced towards the end of the century was a series of 'grotesques'. These were either slip-cast in one piece like the green-glazed cats of Fig. 91, or made by assembling several moulded components, as in the case of the jug shown in Fig. 92. Other articles in the range included, according to a contemporary account, 'grotesque cows and pigs with mouths monstrous as an ogre'. For these there was said to be a 'tremendous demand, which cannot be supplied with sufficient celerity'. Some of these grotesques, which are now fairly rare, were probably stimulated by the modelled stoneware then being produced by Wallace Martin at Southall, although the fashion for earthenware caricatures of cats seems to have been quite widespread about this time.

Standard Patterns and Codes

During the last ten or fifteen years of the nineteenth century Aller Vale introduced several other named styles of decoration. Perhaps the best-known of these was the Motto Ware, which was generally taken up in the present century by the other Torquay potteries and eventually became the typical 'bread-and-butter' product of the local industry. This was characterized by having a little rhyme, precept, or longer quotation scratched through the cream-coloured ground on one side of the article, while the opposite side was usually decorated with what was known locally as 'Scandy'.* The usual 'Scandy' pattern (Fig. 93) consisted of a symmetrical arrangement of brush strokes and spots done in coloured slips, rather like an elaborate 'Prince of Wales's Feathers'. Comparison with Fig. 78 suggests that it was a stylized development of an 'Old Rhodian' motif. However, the word

*The word 'Scandy' has never been seen in print, and is variously pronounced by old pottery workers as 'Scandee', 'Scanda', or 'Scandoo'.

'Scandy' is said to be a corruption of 'Scandinavian', because the style of the painting resembles that found on traditional Norwegian furniture and known as 'rosemaling' (rose painting). Certainly, the example of rosemaling sketched in Fig. iv is very similar to some of the semi-formal Aller floral designs, and it is possible that these were originally included in the general term 'Scandy' (see also p.194).

Mottoes were also provided on articles decorated with the 'Abbots Kerswell' daisy pattern (Fig. 94), but these were usually finished with an amber glaze, whereas the 'Scandy' ware always has a relatively colourless glaze.

It has been said that the inscriptions on early Motto Ware were always done in normal English and that, later, an exaggerated Devonshire dialect was adopted to appeal to the tourist trade. But, in fact, the mottoes were chosen more or less at random from a large repertoire and a visitor who described the Aller Vale Pottery at the end of the nineteenth century noted only one West Country motto amongst all those he saw at the Works. These mottoes (and this holds good for all the other Torquay firms) are always written in what a printer would call 'lower case' letters, and are never joined up as in normal writing script. Although the style of the printing is generally the same for all the potteries the characteristic formation of some of the letters often makes it possible to associate articles with a certain Pottery on this basis alone.

Those articles of Aller Vale pottery that were made from the late 'eighties in batches as stock 'lines' were usually incised underneath with a three-part descriptive code; in addition to the factory mark, which was almost always impressed. The first part of the code consists of a number (which reached four figures in the late 'nineties) that defines the shape of the article. This is followed by a capital letter (usually in script) which describes the general style of the decoration, while a final numeral indicates the particular variant of the style. Thus, 159N.1 is a cream bowl with 'Scandy' decoration; while codes ending in B, followed by a single numeral, will be found on articles decorated with coloured scrolls. Unfortunately, these marks are often partly obscured by the thick glaze which usually covers the bases of the later wares.

Another, but much less common, subject found on Aller Vale ware is a cockerel painted with coloured slips on a cream ground, usually on bowls and with an associated motto (Fig. 95). It is not certain when this pattern was introduced, but since it was given the code N.2 it presumably followed soon after the 'Scandy' design in the 'nineties. The same subject was painted in much greater numbers at the Longpark Pottery from about 1895, and subsequently at Watcombe. However, the Aller Vale cockerel is characterized by having a predominantly green body, usually with ruffled breast feathers, whereas the Longpark birds have smooth, but very puffed-out chests. Probably the motif was copied from the Wemyss Ware made by the Fife Pottery in Scotland, where cockerels were painted in black and in colours from the 1880s. Alternatively, it could have been derived from a French source.

A list of Aller Vale pattern letters with all known sub-divisions is given in Appendix III, but it should be noted that articles were not always marked with a complete code. In particular, both early and late wares (and some moulded articles) were not coded at all, while individually decorated pieces usually have only the shape number incised. At one time it was thought that the pattern letters might have had some alliterative associations with the names by which the designs were known. According to this theory, which was prompted by the fact that green-glazed wares have the code letter G, the 'Abbots Kerswell' pattern was given the letter I because it was evolved under the guidance of an Italian instructor. Similarly the N series could be derived from 'Norwegian'. But many of the other pattern letters, from the considerable number recorded, do not have any obvious connections with likely names. The alternative explanation, that the letters were allocated in alphabetical order, is not entirely satisfactory either, for this would require the green-glazed wares to have been introduced before 'Scandy', which seems unlikely. On the other hand, A.1 was certainly an early pattern, while the Q style of decoration did not appear much before 1900. In the absence of conclusive evidence we must therefore be content with the advice of Mr Arthur Cole, one-time manager of the Watcombe Pottery, who has said: "it's best not to pay too much attention to pattern numbers."

Hexter, Humpherson and Company

By the end of the nineteenth century the Aller Vale Pottery was at the height of its popularity and seemed set for an even more prosperous future. Unfortunately, Mr Phillips died in 1897 and the Works were then bought by Messrs Hexter, Humpherson and Company, who had an extensive business at Kingsteignton, where they worked white clay pits and manufactured tiles and other sanitary fittings. For the next three years the new proprietors allowed the Pottery to continue much as it had before, the only evidence of the change of ownership being that some of the wares were now marked 'ALLER/VALE/H,H & Co.' instead of 'ALLER/VALE/DEVON/ENGLAND'. In 1901, Hexter, Humpherson also acquired the Watcombe Pottery and combined the two businesses under the imposing name: 'The Royal Aller Vale and Watcombe Pottery Company'.* Although Watcombe was larger than Aller Vale the latter was presumably given precedence in the new style by virtue of the 'Royal' prefix. The object of the proprietors was evidently to rationalize the activities of the two firms, but one cannot escape the impression that they were mainly interested in obtaining for the Watcombe factory the right to use the word Royal and to copy the popular Aller Vale wares.

Despite, or possibly because of, the threat of impending decline, the Aller Vale Pottery formed the subject of several articles on country crafts in various national magazines at the turn of the century. In 1900 a Mr Snowden Ward wrote in the *Art-Journal*:

'the native artistic industries of Devonshire — the pottery of Torquay and Barnstaple — are amongst our national assets, part of our British artistic development which we should preserve with the greatest care.'

Of the Pottery itself at this time, Mr Ward continued by saying that:

'. . . with a staff of sixty hands, there is only one man who is not a native of the district, and almost every one came into the works as a boy. Even the manager, Mr Herbert E. Bulley, began as a driver. Aller Vale, with little outside interference,

*But see footnote on p.61.

has developed a series of well-marked shapes, and a few principal styles of decoration . . . There is a constant effort to keep the ideal of good craftsmanship, to avoid machine-made effects, and to encourage originality in the decorators.'

In 1901 an article in *Country Life* also drew attention to the national importance of the Aller Pottery, mentioning that its wares were exported all over the world — to Australia, Canada, and the United States, as well as to Germany and Italy. But the aspect of the business that seems to have impressed the *Country Life* reporter most was: 'the respectable appearance of the workmen, and their civility in explaining the various branches of their craft.'

In 1900 two new styles of decoration were introduced, known respectively as 'Normandy' and 'Crocus' wares. The former was similar in appearance to a style introduced at about the same time at Watcombe, where it was known as 'Green-and-Straw' ware (Fig. 96). Unlike the Watcombe articles, which were made of white clay throughout, the Aller Vale range consisted of existing shapes normally made of red clay dipped in white slip, although a white body was sometimes used. They were then finished by having a translucent green glaze applied to their upper parts and allowed to run down in streaks. The Crocus Ware was quite different, and the nearest that any of the Torquay potteries came to the fashionable Art Nouveau style. All the articles in this range were decorated with bright yellow crocuses and green leaves, done in a semi-natural manner on a dark blue ground. As can be seen from the photograph reproduced in the *Art-Journal* the effect could be quite striking, especially when the shape of the flower repeated the outline of the vase.

By this time the series of decoration codes had been gradually extended, although some of the patterns were so simple that they hardly seem to justify a number. For example, a small jug with the name of a seaside resort painted in cream slip on a green ground has been seen with the code K.6, while another pattern of green leaves alternating with blue flowers is identified as N.6. One of the more distinctive of these late patterns is that believed to be N.9. This is a border design of coloured oval motifs and dots, more suited to the decoration of china than pottery, that has been described as the 'Ladybird' pattern (Fig. 77). It should be noted, however, that this pattern was also done at Longpark, while a similar design has been seen on pottery of German manufacture.

Edwardian Styles

About the beginning of the present century a different method of decoration began to be used on some of the Aller wares. This treatment, which is sometimes distinguished by the code letter Q, involved scratching the outlines of the design through an all-over white ground to show the red body, and then filling in the pattern with translucent glaze colours. Articles finished in this way have a noticeably different and brighter appearance than the more solid-looking slip-decorated wares of the late Victorian period. Indeed, some of the large pitchers of this type (Fig. 97) remind one of the North Devon 'harvest jugs' of a century earlier. The technique was also employed on fairly big vases that were individually decorated with flowers, birds, and dragons, often with borders of large V-shaped motifs associated with what look like fir trees.

In comparison with the last fifteen years of the nineteenth century, few noteworthy patterns were introduced at Aller Vale during the Edwardian era and it is obvious that the Pottery had lost its impetus with the death of Mr Phillips. Nevertheless, the relative scarcity of articles that appear to have been made in the present century may simply be a reflection of a reduction in output during the Hexter, Humpherson period.

One new shape believed to have been introduced in the early 1900s was a conical vase with an unusual fan-shaped rim, pinched into several apertures for holding individual flowers or feathers. It was made in various sizes, and is sometimes found decorated with a slip-painted dolphin (Fig. 98). A larger example has also been seen with a kingfisher brightly painted in pigment colours on a yellow ground. This must have been made, at the latest, soon after the Great War, and its existence is part of the evidence that the 'Kingfisher' pattern was still being developed at that time. Other shapes dating to the beginning of the century included vases and jugs with the cup-shaped, sometimes almost globular, rims that were then fashionable. Many of these will be found with the Hexter, Humpherson mark impressed.

The simple 'Scandy' pattern seems to have gone out of fashion in the twentieth century at Aller, perhaps because it was then being done by most of the other Torquay potteries. In its place one occasionally finds articles painted with a more elaborate design in which the central 'feathers' have been elongated and intertwined to form a narrow figure 8. This style of decoration, sometimes found marked S.3, is more a reversion to (or a continuation of) the 'Old Rhodian' than a development of 'Scandy' and it therefore seems appropriate to describe it as 'Neo-Rhodian'. But perhaps the most tasteful of the early twentieth-century patterns is the repeating floral motif applied to the vase shown in Fig. 99. In common with many Edwardian articles this has the painted mark 'Aller Vale/England', but no pattern code.

During the first two decades of the twentieth century other Torquay potteries were adopting pigment decoration, in the form of landscapes and sailing boats, while slip-painted cottages with scratched outlines were beginning to appear, first at Longpark and then at Watcombe. Yet, although Aller Vale did produce articles decorated with cottages and boats, they are seldom encountered and the designs may have been copied from other firms, possibly as late as 1920. This theory appears to be supported by the absence of pattern codes from such articles.

The usual Aller cottage, as found on small articles, is a single-storey affair, done in slip and sgraffito, with only two windows and a door, just like the later Longpark cottages. Occasionally more substantial buildings are depicted, but these are so much like the usual Watcombe cottages that they could well have been decorated at the St. Marychurch factory on old Aller blanks. The Aller sailing boats, however, resemble those done in slip by the Brewer brothers at Longpark (and by Watcombe), rather than the more detailed pigment-painted 'marine views' of the latter Pottery. The boats themselves are usually no more than a brown triangle for a sail and a black blob for the hull, the typical arrangement including two or three boats and a vague object that may be an island.

Decline and Closure

In 1905 Mr Bulley left Aller to take over the Longpark Pottery in partnership with several other local potters. This was a severe blow for the firm, and one from which it never recovered. The decline of the Aller Pottery, with its all-male staff, was further accelerated by wartime recruitment, and in August 1924 the proprietors closed the Works and transferred production to St. Marychurch. The remaining Aller workmen, including several members of the Bradford family of decorators, were offered employment at Watcombe, but they had to walk or cycle to St. Marychurch and back each day. This involved a round journey of about six miles — in darkness for half the year — an experience that is still remembered by some old potters in the district.

After the closure the Aller Works seem to have been abandoned, and gradually fell into ruins. Mr Phillips's old house, Moor Park, was destroyed by fire about 1928, although the big kilns remained standing until quite recently. Since the Second World War a row of bungalows has been built on the site of the old Pottery, and all that now remains is the former showroom by the side of the main road. This once had a giant teapot on its roof advertising Aller Vale wares, but today it serves a more prosaic purpose as the offices of a building firm. Fortunately, the earlier business is not entirely forgotten, for the bus-stop outside the building is still generally known as 'The Potteries'.

ALLER VALE MARKS

(i) *Factory Marks*. Most articles appear to have been marked, although on early articles with unglazed bases the mark was often made illegible by handling before firing. Similarly, on glazed articles, the marks may be partly obscured by slip or glaze.

33. ΦΙΛΕΩ ΙΠΠΟΝ   Early impressed mark, mentioned by Llewellynn Jewitt as having been used in conjunction with a horse's head, but not seen by the present writers. c.1880?

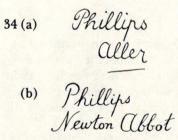

34 (a)   *Phillips Aller*   Incised mark used on early Art wares. c.1881—c.1887.

(b)   *Phillips Newton Abbot*   Alternative form of (a).

35. MADE IN DEVON   Impressed mark seen on early glazed wares attributed to the Aller Pottery. c.1881—c.1887.

36. AllerVale   Incised mark. c.1885.

37.   ALLER VALE

Impressed mark, on one line, with serifs to the letters. Not usually found on articles decorated with a coded pattern. c.1887 – c.1897.

38 (a)   **ALLER VALE DEVON ENGLAND**

The usual impressed mark on articles decorated with standard coded patterns: e.g. 'Scandy', scrolls, etc. c.1891 – 1924.

(b)   ALLER VALE

Simple version of (a). First used about 1887, but employed intermittently up to 1924, sometimes with 'ENGLAND' separately impressed.

39.   ALLER VALE H, H & Co.

A version of No. 38 used for a few years after 1897, when the Pottery was acquired by Messrs Hexter, Humpherson & Co.

40.   *Aller Vale England*

Painted mark, usually including 'England' or 'Made in England'. c.1900 – 1924.

(ii) *Pattern Numbers.* For an explanation of the numbers and letters often found scratched on the bases of Aller Vale articles see p.123 and Appendix III. Shape numbers reached about 1400 by the year 1900, but were not much used subsequently. Early articles, and many late ones, have only a factory mark.

(iii) *Potters' Marks.* No craftsmen's marks have been identified on Aller Vale pottery.

Section Five

LONGPARK

Plate VI. Large Longpark vase decorated with a version of the
'Kingfisher' pattern, showing the bird perched on a branch instead of diving.
Height: 355 mm (14 in). c. 1930. (See Fig. 122(b) for a photograph of the
mark.)

When rosy plumlets tuft the larch,
  And rarely pipes the mounted thrush;
Or underneath the barren bush
Flits by the sea-blue bird of March.

Tennyson: *In Memoriam*.

The frequent changes of name and ownership of what is generally known as the Longpark Pottery are typical more of the small Staffordshire 'pot banks' of the early nineteenth century than of the other, relatively stable, Torquay firms. And, if one believes the semi-fictional account in Eden Phillpotts' novel *Brunel's Tower*, this factory was indeed established by two Staffordshire potters, named George Easterbrook and Paul Pitts, in a derelict building that had originally been erected to serve as a pumping station for I.K. Brunel's ill-fated 'atmospheric' railway.

However, although the setting of Phillpotts' story was real enough, and the implied period (some time in the 1880s) vaguely correct, the names Easterbrook and Pitts were evidently provided by the novelist, for the first reference to a pottery in the Long Park district of Torquay, in Kelly's Directory of Devonshire for 1883, gives the names of the proprietors as Messrs. Crutchlow and Ridley. Nevertheless, Phillpotts was probably correct in saying that the founders of the Longpark Pottery hailed from Staffordshire, for it seems

135

that Crutchlow and Ridley were former employees of the Watcombe Pottery who had been recruited from 'The Potteries' when the St. Marychurch firm was established in the early 'seventies. In that case they may well have been obliged to set up on their own when Watcombe was temporarily closed between 1883 and 1884.

The Terracotta Works

In the 1883 directory the firm is simply described as 'The Longpark Pottery', under the heading 'Terra Cotta Manufacturers'. Little is known of the early products of the business, but they are believed to have consisted mainly or wholly of unglazed terracotta wares of the general type that had been made for the past twelve years at Watcombe and, from 1875, at the near-by works of the Torquay Terra-Cotta Company at Hele Cross. Vases of 'pilgrim bottle' shape and circular wall plaques were then very popular, decorated with oil painting or sold as blanks for amateurs to paint on, and it is probable that articles of this kind formed the bulk of the output.

Fig. 100(a) shows three examples of painted Longpark plaques, one decorated with a river scene and the others with flowers, and all made from a fine light-coloured terracotta. The largest of these, which is 14 inches across, is priced on the back in pencil at 1/11d, followed by the letters 'byc'. Since plaques of this size would sell at that time for several shillings when decorated, it must be supposed that this one was sold as a blank. Also, since the letters can be interpreted as an abbreviation for 'Brown and Yellow Chrysanthemums', it is possible that the plaque was supplied with the outlines of the flowers already printed on it, as a guide.

Although marked examples of early Longpark terracotta are seldom encountered, all the plaques illustrated bear the crisply impressed circular mark illustrated in Fig. 100(b). As can be seen, this contains the names 'LONGPARK/ TORQUAY' in the centre, surrounded by the words 'TERRA COTTA — WORKS' in smaller lettering, the blank consisting of a raised sector where a word has obviously been engraved out of the die. It might be thought that the missing word was

'ART', or possibly 'CLAY', in imitation of the original name of the Watcombe Pottery, which was 'The Watcombe Terra-Cotta Clay Co.' However, the width of the blank sector indicates that the word contained between four and five letters and must therefore have been something else. The mystery was eventually solved by the six-inch Ordnance Survey map of 1889, which identifies the Pottery buildings with the unexpected legend 'Longpark Terra Cotta China Works'. Evidently the blank space in the stamp originally contained the word 'CHINA', the narrow letter I accounting for the uncertainty as to the number of letters. It is difficult to understand how such a confusing name came to be adopted. The only explanation seems to be that the products of the Pottery were colloquially described as 'china', despite their colour, in the same way that in some parts of Britain table wares of all kinds are still referred to as 'delph'. But it must have been realized that the name was misleading for the die to have been modified, and it would be interesting to know whether any examples of Longpark pottery exist which have the unmodified mark.

In the 1889 Directory the name of the firm is given as the 'Longpark Fine Art Terra Cotta Company', a Mr Taylor having replaced Mr Crutchlow in the partnership. This entry is repeated in the 1893 edition, but by 1897 a Mr Ralph Willott had taken the place of Mr Ridley. Nevertheless, these dates must be treated with some reserve, and are probably later than the actual events, since the Directories were only published at intervals of about four years.

The Brewer Brothers

From the late 'nineties until about 1905 the Pottery was operated by Mr Willott in partnership with the brothers William and James Brewer, who had previously assisted their father Henry Brewer in his small Pottery at the back of Broomhill Cottages, half a mile away (see p.167). According to the Directory of 1902 the firm then described itself simply as 'Brewer Brothers', but with the difference that the address was given as 'Shiphay Collaton, Cockington', instead of the previous 'Newton Road, St. Mary Church'. From this it might be concluded that the Willott/Brewer firm did not operate on the same site as the earlier partnerships, because the hamlet of Shiphay Collaton is some three-quarters of a mile off the Newton Road and on the opposite side to Brunel's Tower. However, the real reason for the apparent change of address was simply a revision of the boundary between the parishes of St. Mary Church and Cockington, as can be seen by comparing the Ordnance Survey map of 1906 with that of 1889.

It is significant that the 1902 Directory lists Brewer Brothers under 'Potters', whereas the earlier partnerships had always been under the heading 'Terra-cotta Manufacturers'. In the closing years of the nineteenth century the older Torquay potteries, following the lead given by Aller Vale, had been obliged by changing fashion to abandon terracotta in favour of thrown and glazed wares. It is not surprising, therefore, to find that the Longpark Works also began to make glazed earthenware at this time, and the Directory entry clearly reflects this change.

Although the Brewer brothers produced some fine quality pottery, and introduced several distinctive styles of decoration, their products have remained unrecognized and ignored for the past seventy years. This is because the marks applied to the bases of the articles were so faintly scratched that they were all but obliterated by the thick glaze. The mark generally used was 'BREWER/Longpark/Torquay', and many apparently anonymous articles of pottery with obvious Torquay characteristics will, on close inspection, be found to have this mark. But to see it requires a great deal of concentration and just the right light. In fact, it is difficult to understand why the firm bothered to go on marking its wares with what was virtually invisible writing.* The answer may well have been that, in a business as competitive as the Torquay pottery industry, you didn't want to make it too obvious to the firm up the road that you were copying their ideas! The absence of a clear mark also made it easier for a shopkeeper to pass off your wares as those of a better-known Pottery.

*A similar style of marking was used at the Torquay Pottery until about 1922, but the products of the two firms can usually be distinguished by other means.

The pottery made by the Brewers at Longpark is similar in general appearance and finish to the slip-decorated wares previously made at Broomhill, and is notable for its clean, bright, appearance and good glaze. It was orginally made from a clay that fired to a pale peach-red and, for this reason, is often attributed to Aller Vale. Identification of the firm's early pottery is not helped by the fact that it included a great deal of motto ware decorated with the Aller Vale 'Scandy' design and even marked with the corresponding N.1 pattern code.

One of the most attractive of the Brewers' decorative subjects, however, was the coloured cockerel associated with pattern code N.2. Good examples are not often encountered, but Fig. 101 shows a twin-handled mug painted with this design in bright slip colours on a cream ground. The base carries the faintly scratched Brewer Longpark mark, together with '26N.2' in more boldly scored characters; while the ends of the handles are impressed down to the level of the body with the outline of a leaf, in the manner of some traditional-style Aller Vale wares. The 'Cockerel' design was also done with the bird painted mainly in black, when it was known as the N.3 pattern (Fig. 102). Both coloured and black cockerels were usually accompanied by a scratched motto, sometimes with the words 'Good Morning' in addition.

As mentioned in Section 4, there is some doubt as to which firm introduced the 'Cockerel' design to the Torquay potteries, for examples also occur on articles bearing Aller Vale and Watcombe marks. Since Aller Vale originated the N.1 pattern it might be supposed that it also introduced N.2 and N.3. But, while examples of the 'Coloured Cockerel' are occasionally found on Aller Vale pottery made in the 1890s, no 'Black Cockerel' has been seen on an article bearing an Aller mark. It thus seems that the Brewers may have been responsible for N.3, and that they simply extended what was, by then, an almost universal decoration code, but with their own shape numbers prefixed. Even if they did not, the 'Black Cockerel' will always be associated with Longpark because so much of its later pottery was decorated with this pattern.

Apart from what may be regarded as their 'standard' designs, the Brewers also did other slip-decorated patterns which are less frequently encountered. It is understood that some of the decoration, which is always pleasantly composed, was done by Mr James Brewer himself, who shared his time between this activity and travelling for the firm. A typical example is the all-over leaf design shown in Fig. 103. This is painted in white slip with brown shading on a pale green ground under an amber glaze, but its pattern number, if it had one, is not known. Other botanical subjects attributed to this firm include a Canterbury Bell flower painted in blue and green.

The Later Brewer Wares

From about 1900 the Brewers began to use a different clay for some of their pottery. This fired to a dark chocolate-coloured body, containing minute white specks, that was to become typical of Longpark in the second decade of the present century. It should be noted, though, that the contemporary Hart and Moist Pottery in Exeter used a very similar speckled dark body and it is often difficult to distinguish between unmarked wares of the two potteries. In such cases it is helpful to remember that the Brewer glaze is usually much better than that of the Exeter firm. According to Eden Phillpotts, the clay was originally dug adjacent to the Works, and it is quite possible that the light-coloured material was found close at hand, although there is now no obvious sign of a clay-pit. The dark clay probably came from another site on the opposite side of the Newton Road, now filled in and serving as the car park of a public house, which became the main source of supply for the Pottery in later years.

One of the most popular of the standard patterns used by the Brewers to decorate their later, dark-bodied, wares was a slip-painted fishing boat with a single mast and brown sails. This was typically shown ploughing through a green sea, leaving a wake of white foam, and was done on a whole range of articles, including tea-services, mugs, jugs, beakers, and tobacco jars (Fig. 104). The opposite side of the article was usually provided with a short sgraffito inscription appropriate to its purpose, e.g. 'Tobacco, Help Yersel'. Another type of slip decoration introduced in the early years of the present century showed a thatched cottage set between trees and approached by a winding path. Like the sailing-boat, this pattern was generally accompanied by a suitable motto, or the name of the place where the article was intended to be sold, and Fig. 105 shows a Brewer tea-service decorated in this manner.

The chief interest in these two patterns lies in the fact that they were introduced at Longpark some years before the subjects were copied by any of the other Torquay potteries. Watcombe, for example, did not advertise its 'Marine Views' until the beginning of the Great War and, although cottages appear in some of that Pottery's topographic decoration of the same period, its more famous Cottage Ware dates from towards the end of the War. The Brewers therefore deserve the credit for the inception of several of the most popular styles of decoration used on twentieth century Torquay pottery. It should be noted, however, that since the sailing ships done by other potteries were mostly painted in pigment colours, a slip-painted boat is usually indicative of Longpark manufacture.

Another type of pottery produced at Longpark in the early 1900s was decorated in imitation of the Aller Vale 'Normandy' wares. This had the dark body dipped in white slip, with a subsequent coat of clear glaze. Before the final firing the upper part of each piece was dipped into a translucent green glaze, which was allowed to run down in streaks over the body. A four-necked vase decorated in this way is shown in Fig. 96. Although a typical Aller Vale shape, this particular Longpark version has frilled, instead of plain, rims to the spouts.

Apart from the wares themselves, and the names of the proprietors, little is really known about the Brewer business. Despite the fact that it produced some attractive pottery during its few years' occupancy of the Longpark Works it must ultimately have proved unprofitable, for about 1905 the partnership was dissolved and the two Brewer brothers removed to St. Marychurch (see p.169).

The Limited Company

After the departure of the Brewers there was a complete change of ownership at Longpark. The first mention of the new firm occurs in Kelly's Directory of 1906, where it is listed as 'The Longpark Pottery Company Limited', of Newton Road, Cockington, Torquay. Despite its new legal status the business was still very much a partnership of the old kind, for it was formed by six local potters who each put up £50 or £100 to take over the Works. The Directory gives the name of the Company Secretary as Herbert Edward Bulley, who had previously been Manager of the Aller Vale Pottery for many years. Other subscribers, who are said to have come from Watcombe, included two Skinner brothers, a Mr Bond (decorator), and a Mr Causeley (thrower). The sixth person was the fireman, possibly a Mr Blackler from Aller Vale.

Registration as a Limited Company evidently provided the Longpark Pottery with much-needed stability, for it retained this status for the remainder of its existence, and it is this firm which is usually meant by people in Torquay when they speak of *the* Longpark Pottery. Indeed, there seems to be no ceramics reference book which even mentions the presence of a Pottery at Longpark before 1905.

As far as is known, the Limited Company never made terracotta, but concentrated on the manufacture of small glazed pieces, of the kind introduced by the Brewers, that were formed by throwing, moulding, or jolleying. These included all the usual shapes: cream jugs and bowls, tea-services, and vases of various kinds; together with articles such as hatpin holders, which were a speciality of the Torquay potteries, and sweetmeat dishes. Decorated plaques and plates with mottoes or longer inscriptions were also popular at this time (Fig. 107). These wares generally have an even darker body than those of the late Brewer period, and it may well have been that the clay was deliberately tinted to suit contemporary taste.

The styles of decoration applied to the pottery of the Bulley period were mostly copied from Aller Vale and Watcombe, together with their pattern numbers (Fig. 106). They included a version of the 'Renaissance Scroll' design, usually done on waisted vases with skewed handles, as well as the ever-popular

'Scandy', the latter always in combination with mottoes or longer inscriptions. The firm also continued the Brewers' sailing boat design, but in a simplified form with a single lug sail, instead of the fore-and-aft sails sometimes found on early versions. A characteristic over-border decoration on Longpark pottery of this period, and subsequently, consisted of a series of kidney-shaped blobs of slip, usually blue or green but sometimes red or orange. Other potteries, notably Watcombe and Aller Vale, also decorated the rims of plates and vases with coloured spots, but these were generally circular. The ground colours used on Longpark slip-ware were mostly cream or dark green, and the cream grounds were frequently bordered with green. The borders themselves were either solidly painted, or put on with an air brush so that the colour gradually faded out. Less frequently, blue or grey are found as border colours.

Longpark colours of the Bulley period often look colder and greyer than those of other Torquay potteries. This is usually attributed to the firm's practice of firing at a higher temperature than elsewhere; but other factors, such as the dark body and the thin glaze, combined to make many of the Longpark wares of the late Edwardian period even more sombre than their Watcombe equivalents.

In addition to the standard designs mentioned, articles of Longpark pottery are occasionally found decorated in slip with a romantic scene of a ruined abbey by the side of a river and silhouetted against an evening sky. The better examples, such as the tall jug shown in Fig. 108, are quite effective and represent the only known attempt by a Torquay pottery to represent the tonal gradations of a landscape in the difficult medium of coloured slip. It is not surprising, therefore, to find that many of these pieces have the letters 'S.S.', presumed to be the initials of one of the Skinner brothers, scratched after the shape number instead of the usual impersonal decoration code.

Another distinctive feature of Longpark pottery made just before the Great War is the way the ends of the handles are stamped with the outline of an acanthus leaf. Like the Brewer and Watcombe handles these were sometimes spread out right down to the body of the pot, although a later method of shaping produced the leaf outline on top of a small pad, rather like the impression of a seal on soft wax.

The Royal Tormohun Pottery

The products of the Longpark Pottery Company from 1905 until about 1910 were usually impressed 'LONGPARK/ TORQUAY' in block capitals. However, collectors of Torquay pottery will come across articles which are identical in all respects to the Longpark wares just described, except that they have the word 'TORMOHUN' included in the mark, sometimes in association with the word 'LONGPARK' (Figs. 109 & 110). The earliest form of these marks was a separate stamp with the words 'TORMOHUN/WARE', in addition to the normal 'LONGPARK/TORQUAY' mark. In other, slightly later, versions the words are variously combined in a single stamp as 'TORMOHUN/WARE/TORQUAY' or 'TORMOHUN/LONGPARK/TORQUAY'. There is no doubt that these articles were made by, or for, a firm which was listed in the 1910 edition of Kelly's Directory as the 'Royal Tormohun Pottery Co. Ltd. (Art)', with the address: 'Long Park, Newton Road, Torquay'. Since this edition has a separate entry for the 'Longpark Pottery Co. Ltd.', it must be assumed that these two Limited Companies were legally distinct firms. Unfortunately, the records in the Register of Dissolved Companies at the Department of Trade have been destroyed, and despite extensive enquiries nothing more is known for certain about the Royal Tormohun Pottery.*

The lack of evidence of any other pottery Works in the Longpark district suggests that the Tormohun Pottery was either a sub-division of the Longpark Pottery, or shared its facilities on some other basis. In either case one would expect that Tormohun Ware would have been a different kind of pottery to that produced by the earlier business. A third possibility is that the Tormohun firm was simply a marketing

*Until the present century the area now known as Torquay was described in the directories as the 'Parish of Torquay and Tormoham'. The latter word, variously spelt, referred to the upper part of the district, including Torre and Long Park.

organization for the Longpark Pottery. There is also the question as to how the word 'Royal' came to be included in the name of the new company — usually an indication of patronage by royalty. The key to the mystery probably lies in the word 'Art' added in brackets to the name of the firm in the Directory entry. This implies that the intention was to produce pottery of a more artistic or ornamental kind than the run-of-the-mill useful articles that formed the bulk of Longpark's output. But the fact that the Tormohun firm went on supplying Longpark-type wares (if, indeed, it ever had a separate existence), indicates that there was some setback which prevented this intention from being realized, at least for several years. This is confirmed by the absence of any reference to the Royal Tormohun Pottery in Directories after 1910, so the firm could only have existed for a few years before the Great War.

One method of decoration which seems to have been used only about the time of the Tormohun Pottery, but is found on both 'Longpark' and 'Tormohun' wares, is represented by the small vase of Fig. 111. This has a coloured view of Cockington Village which, at first sight, resembles the topographic faience painting done by the Watcombe Pottery at that time and, to a lesser extent, by Longpark itself. However, closer inspection shows that the outlines and title of the scene have been applied by transfer printing in black, and the trees and buildings roughly filled in with pigment colours. Evidently this was an attempt to imitate the appearance of hand painting by cheaper means, but its chief interest now is that it is one of the few instances of the use of transfer printing on Torquay pottery in the twentieth century.

Another type of Longpark article, which at the time of writing has only been seen with a Tormohun mark, is the little figure of a pig playing a concertina illustrated in Fig. 112. This is unusual for Longpark, not only as a subject, but because it is slip-cast from white clay and finished with a translucent green glaze. Evidently, it was intended to compete with the Aller Vale and Watcombe grotesques introduced at a slightly earlier date, and the example shown may well have been one of a series or group of similar articles.

K

The Royal Longpark Pottery

In the 1914 Directories there are still two entries for potteries at Longpark: the original Longpark Pottery Co. Ltd., and a firm described as the 'Royal Longpark Pottery Co. Ltd. (Art)'. The retention of the words 'Royal' and 'Art' in the name of the new firm suggests that it was really the Royal Tormohun Pottery in a new guise; possibly a result of a reorganization of the Longpark Company following the appointment of Mr R.H. Skinner as Company Secretary in succession to Mr Bulley.

Although there had been little about the old Tormohun Ware, apart from its marks, to distinguish it from the other Longpark products, the articles made by the Royal Longpark Pottery were not only distinctive, but in a class by themselves in comparison with the products of most other Torquay firms at that time. Evidently, some arrangements had been made by 1914 for the separate production, with the Longpark Works, of studio-type pottery of a higher artistic quality than the ordinary souvenir wares. Yet, despite the precedent of 'Tormohun *Ware*' (the word 'Ware' generally implying hand-made pottery with a deliberate Arts-and-Crafts character) these articles were simply marked 'Longpark Torquay'. The only unusual feature of the mark was that the words were incised by hand in bold script, instead of being impressed with a die or rubber-stamped.

The Royal Longpark Pottery was established at a difficult time, just before the outbreak of war, but it remained in existence for some ten years. Initially, the articles produced were based on established forms, but with more interesting decoration than the ordinary slip wares. In particular, much of the early Art pottery was finished with a combination of coloured slips and coloured translucent glazes in the style previously developed by C.H. Brannam at Barnstaple. Fig. 113, for example, shows a four-necked globular vase, of typical Torquay shape, decorated with white slip painted to resemble a swag of fabric supported on rings. This has a brown body and is finished in a flown glaze of turquoise blue colour. But the most significant feature of this vase is the number '39', heavily scored on the base after the words 'Longpark/

Torquay', for this was the number given by the Longpark Pottery Co. Ltd. to all vases of this shape, regardless of size or decoration. Its presence on this piece is therefore additional evidence, if any were needed, that the Royal Longpark Pottery operated as a separate workshop, or studio, on the premises of the parent firm for the decoration of a superior class of ornamental pottery. Presumably its registration as a Limited Company was largely an accounting convenience.

Another article finished with translucent blue glaze over a brown body is the ornamental candlestick of Fig. 114. This is decorated in relief with a dragon that has been separately moulded and applied to the column and then touched up with various coloured slips to emphasize its mouth, teeth, and claws. Dragons and lizards were a favourite form of relief ornamentation on Barnstaple pottery and, although the Brannam candlestick illustrated in Fig. 94 of our *Victorian Art Pottery* is decorated with Art Nouveau motifs, the two articles are otherwise identical in colouring and decorative treatment.

Yet another example of Royal Longpark pottery that combines several techniques to produce an article that might, in the absence of a mark, be attributed to a Barnstaple firm is the twin-handled mug of Fig. 116. This is made of white clay and is decorated with a frog entwined in water weed, carved and painted in coloured slips within a diamond-shaped panel. The ground inside the diamond is stippled to a rough surface and the outside of the piece is finished in a blue-green translucent glaze. In addition to 'Longpark Torquay' this mug has the number '26' incised on its base and, as might be expected, is the same size and shape as the Brewer mug with this number illustrated in Fig. 101.

A final, later, example of Longpark Art pottery is the substantial bowl illustrated in Fig. 115. This is nine inches in diameter, and probably dates to the early 'twenties. It is thickly potted from a dark brown clay and decorated on the outside of the rim with applied leaves and flowers (probably roses). The leaves and the lower part of the bowl are sponged with green pigment and the whole article is covered with an amber glaze. A circular wall plaque has also been seen with this style of decoration, the roses complemented by a verse neatly trailed in white slip.

There is no suggestion that the articles produced by the Royal Longpark Pottery were unique, in the sense that they were never exactly duplicated, as was the case at Doulton's Art Studios in Lambeth in the nineteenth century. Several examples of the vase of Fig. 113 have been seen, and it is probable that articles were decorated in small batches to the same pattern. Nevertheless, these Art wares are much scarcer than pottery bearing the normal mark of the parent firm — perhaps only one out of every fifty encountered.

The similarity of the early Longpark Art wares to pottery produced at the turn of the century by the Barnstaple factories suggests that the person responsible for decoration at the Royal Longpark Pottery had been trained at one of the North Devon firms. Although there is, at present, no documentary evidence to support this theory, it is possible that the individual concerned was the Mr (Tom?) Lemon who went into partnership with Mr Harry Crute about 1922 to set up the Daison Pottery (see p.173). If so, it would explain why the Royal Longpark Pottery ceased to operate soon after this date, and is not mentioned in later Directories.

The Longpark of Brunel's Tower

Eden Phillpotts' novel of the Longpark Pottery was first published in 1915, and the events described are set mainly in the period just before the Great War. One local potter who spent all his working life at Watcombe and Longpark maintains that the book describes the early days of the latter firm 'just as it happened'. Certainly, Phillpotts gives the names (fictitious, of course) of six men, in the more responsible positions, who appear to correspond to the six founder members of the real Limited Company. But, although the novelist was correct in saying that about forty persons worked at the Pottery, there is no evidence to support his reference to women decorators at this time. Except, perhaps, for a few girls in the office or packing shed, all the employees would have been men or boys. Also contrary to the description of the Works in *Brunel's Tower*, the tall chimney of the original pumping station, in the form of an Italian campanile, was not used for the flues of the kilns. These were, in fact, conventional five-mouth bottle kilns of the type used at the other Torquay potteries and, although Phillpotts refers to four kilns, local sources of information indicate that there were only two at the time the firm closed down. It is possible, however, that the chimney was used for the steam engine that originally drove the machinery.

It is also interesting to find that the novel describes a separate studio in the Works where one of the partners (Mr Pitts) modelled and decorated the better-quality articles. This seems to be a reference to the Royal Longpark side of the business, especially as there is a detailed account of how Mr Pitts moulded and assembled the dragons used to decorate articles like the candlestick of Fig. 114:

'I made moulds of this favourite dragon and reproduce him wing by wing and claw by claw. The art is to make the dragon part of the pot he belongs to, and order his turns and twists to chime with the lines of the pot.'

Mr Pitts is also said to have modelled figures, but there is no evidence that Longpark ever made anything of this kind. Another of his creations 'during a lighter moment' was '. . . a little dish, or ash-tray, in the shape of a flat-fish. Upon it were written the words "A pla(i)ce for everything".' This article, with the word 'ashes' substituted for 'everything' was certainly made by Longpark (see Fig. 117); but whether it was devised before, or as a result of, Phillpotts' description is hard to say.

Many of the types of decoration said to have been applied to 'Brunel Faience' can be found on Longpark pottery made during the years between 1910 and 1915. Of these, the following may be mentioned in particular:

Daffodils. These flowers were painted in a natural style, using yellow and green slips over a dark green ground, and will be found on ornamental pieces of various shapes. When well done, this style of decoration can be very pleasing. Fig. 118 shows a typical example on a four-necked globular vase, but it should be remembered that this subject was also done in the same manner at Watcombe.

Roses. Just before the Great War the fashion for slip

decoration on the wares of the Torquay potteries was dying out in favour of more colourful patterns done underglaze in pigment colours. Roses were a popular decorative motif at this time and were painted by several of the Torquay firms. At the Longpark Pottery they were done in crimson on a white ground, usually with sprayed green borders, and it is interesting to note that identical decoration can be found on articles marked 'LONGPARK/TORQUAY' and 'TORMOHUN/WARE/TORQUAY' (Figs. 110 & 119).

Thistles and Shamrocks. Small articles were decorated simply, almost perfunctorily, with a thistle flower in green and violet, or a spray of green shamrock leaves, on a white ground. These were evidently intended for supply to customers in, or from, Scotland and Ireland as the national equivalents of the Rose pattern.

Sailing Boats. The Brewer design was still being produced up to at least the time of the Great War, although the slip was much thinner and may only have been a thick pigment colour. In *Brunel's Tower* this pattern is attributed to Mr Easterbrook's daughter Joanna.

Cock o' the North. According to Phillpotts, the Longpark Pottery made large numbers of articles decorated with what he calls the 'Cock o' the North' for Scottish customers. It is assumed that this refers to the popular Black Cockerel pattern, although the description 'Cock of the North' is a common name for the brambling, not a barnyard fowl. A similar subject believed to have been painted about this time, but less common than the Black Cockerel, was a large black hen surrounded by small white chickens in a green field.

Apart from these identifiable types of ware, other kinds of pottery and decorative patterns described in *Brunel's Tower* have not been found with a Longpark mark or, in some cases, with any other Torquay mark. It is possible, of course, that Eden Phillpotts ascribed to the Longpark Pottery several types of ware which were actually made by other firms, or had been made in the past. Nevertheless, two styles of decoration described in his book in great detail: the 'Ups and Downs' and the 'Peacock's Feather' seem to have been products of the novelist's own imagination.

Longpark in the 'Twenties

Mr R.H. (Bob) Skinner, who had taken over from Mr Bulley about 1913 as Secretary of the Longpark Pottery Company was, in fact, a managing director of the firm, and in this capacity he ran the business for nearly thirty years. The description 'a managing director' is used rather than '*the* Managing Director' because, although Mr Skinner is always regarded as having been the head of the firm, some large articles of pottery can be found stamped with the names of *three* 'Joint Managing Directors' (see Fig. 122(b)). From this evidence it would appear that Mr Skinner was the most senior of a triumvirate, of which the other members were Mr George W. Bond and Mr Frederick H. Blackler.

Mr Skinner's assumption of control coincided with the abandonment of impressed factory marks, and for the next twenty years the ordinary wares were usually marked with a rubber stamp 'LONGPARK/TORQUAY' in black under the glaze. Although there were slight variations in the style of marking it is difficult to date Longpark pottery made during the second and third decades of the present century to within a few years from the mark alone. For this reason there is less certainty as to the sequence of the decorative patterns introduced after about 1915 than before this date.

Longpark wares with a rubber-stamped mark often have a pattern number painted in black on the base. The initial number consists of two or three figures and refers only to the shape of the article, or a set of articles such as a tea-service. The variety of these numbers is quite limited, giving the impression that they were standard popular designs; the unpopular ones having been discarded, or not used for some other reason. When an article is decorated with a design of Aller Vale origin, or derivation, i.e. 'Scandy' (N.1), or a cockerel (N.2 or N.3), then the decoration code is usually painted after the shape number. However, articles finished with patterns introduced in Mr Skinner's time, after 1915, are never marked with a decoration code.

During the early 'twenties Longpark produced a range of articles decorated with brightly-coloured butterflies on a streaky mauve-pink ground (Fig. 120). The articles finished in this way included tea-services, bowls, vases, hatpin holders, and small baskets. There seems to have been a vogue for butterflies at this time, for they were done both in relief and painted by the Torquay Pottery at Hele Cross, and at the Daison Pottery. The Longpark butterflies, however, may be distinguished by the fact that they are boldly painted in white, yellow, and orange, with black outlines and spots, while the articles themselves have the fashionable black rims of the period. Some of these wares are unusual in that their bases have been left unglazed,* in contrast to most Longpark pottery of this period, which was highly glazed all over and fired on stilts. Another peculiarity is that the mark is occasionally printed as 'TORQUAY/LONGPARK' instead of the usual sequence.

Another contemporary pattern on the same mauve ground involved sprays of large pink flowers amongst green leaves, also done in underglaze pigment colours and outlined in black (Fig. 119). This was an almost exact copy of the 'Alexandra rose' design painted on articles at the Torquay Pottery, the only differences being that the Hele Cross roses have more conspicuous thorns on their stems and the ground colour is redder than at Longpark. However, unlike Hele Cross, Longpark never combined scratched mottoes with coloured grounds, presumably because the lettering did not show up as effectively as on a white or cream ground.

Cockerels and Kingfishers

During the inter-war years the output of the Longpark Pottery was second only to that of Watcombe amongst the Torquay firms, while the quality of its work was generally up to the standard set by the larger factory. On the other hand,

*The Daison Pottery was the only other Torquay firm that regularly made glazed wares with a 'dry' base in the first half of the present century.

Longpark had a smaller range of patterns than Watcombe, preferring to concentrate on a few popular designs and a wide variety of articles. The 'Black Cockerel', in particular, remained very popular as a subject for the decoration of useful wares such as tea-services and candlesticks, usually in association with an appropriate motto (Fig. 121). This pattern (N.3), which was known at the Pottery as the 'cock crowing' design, is now regarded as one of the two most characteristic Longpark styles of decoration. Occasionally one finds a piece made in the 'twenties or 'thirties, marked 'N.2', with a few dabs of colour on the wings of the bird to justify the different pattern number, but the quality of the painting does not stand comparison with the original Brewer 'Coloured Cockerel'. Incidentally, candlesticks seem to have been a Longpark speciality, and were made in a variety of shapes and sizes.

By comparison, the 'Cottage-and-Motto' pattern does not seem to have been made in any great quantity at Longpark after the Great War. In style, these later cottages are more like the Watcombe version than the Brewer cottages of two or three decades earlier. However, the Longpark cottages may be distinguished by the fact that they are single-storey cabins with only one or two windows and a door, instead of the two-storey buildings usually depicted at Watcombe.

The pattern that is most closely identified with the Longpark Pottery during the inter-war years, however, is the 'Kingfisher' design (Plate VI & Fig. 122(a)). Like sailing boats, this was done by most of the Torquay potteries and, like the Willow pattern on early nineteenth century Staffordshire earthenware, has several basic elements which are always present, although variations occur in arrangement and colouring. This style of decoration has a bright blue ground all over the outside of the body, and on this is depicted a single kingfisher, usually diving into a pool of water. The bird is painted underglaze in pigment colours, mainly shades of blue and green, with a black outline and touches of yellow and orange on its feathers. Overhead is the forked branch of a tree, sometimes bearing pink blossoms; on either side are painted green rushes to fill the remaining space, while a few strokes of white slip represent water-lily flowers. It has been said that the 'Kingfisher' design was originated by Mr Hunt, a decorator at the Watcombe Pottery; but, although it was certainly done at that factory, most of the articles with this decoration to be found today bear a Longpark mark.

It is difficult to say where the 'Kingfisher' pattern really originated. In all probability it evolved gradually from the 'exotic birds' of the eighteenth century china factories, through the elaborate bird compositions done by painters from the Staffordshire Potteries working at Watcombe and Hele Cross at the end of the nineteenth century. The enamelled 'Torquay' jug of Fig. 49, for example, has most of the essential features of the final pattern, except that the bird is a swallow and the background is plain terracotta, while a pair of kingfishers form the subject of the oil-painted decoration on the Watcombe dish of Fig. 17. In the present century the immediate precursor of the fully-developed 'Kingfisher' pattern seems to be the version that appears on the bowl of Fig. 136, which was made at the Bovey Tracey Art Pottery in 1922. This has all the characteristics of the final version, except that the ground is cream, rather than blue. Since blue grounds had been generally adopted by the Torquay potteries by 1923 it may be concluded that the 'Kingfisher' pattern, as represented by the articles shown in Fig. 122(a), dates from about this year.

Blue grounds, in various shades, had of course been used by the Aller Vale Pottery in the nineteenth century, but their reintroduction in the 'twenties could well have been due to the impression created by Maeterlinck's play *The Blue Bird*. Although this classic was written in 1909 it did not become generally known on the English side of the Channel until after the Great War. The title then caught the imagination of the public, and blue-birds provided not only a theme for popular songs and a name for commercial products, but a fashionable decorative motif besides. As a result, blue birds of several kinds were painted by most of the Torquay potteries. The Daison Pottery, in particular, produced some attractive vases decorated with blue-tits (Fig. 128), while the 'Kingfisher' pattern was copied by firms as far afield as Weston-super-Mare. A stylized version of the subject can also be found on articles made by Carter, Stabler, and Adams at the Poole Pottery.

It is interesting to note that on individual articles, like

teapots, the Longpark kingfisher is always shown diving from right to left. At Watcombe the reverse direction seems to have been preferred, except that at both factories pairs of vases had the birds diving in opposite directions for symmetry. Although the 'Kingfisher' pattern remained popular at Longpark for the remainder of the firm's existence other blue-ground subjects were also produced during the 'twenties and 'thirties. Typical of these is the vase shown in Fig. 119, decorated with an iris in blue, yellow, and green. Like most of the Longpark wares of this period, this article has a medium red body, but not of such good quality as the early Brewer pottery.

The Final Decade

During the Second World War the Longpark Pottery was obliged to close down because it had no export trade and therefore could not obtain a licence to make decorated wares. After the War the Works were acquired by the owners of the Watcombe Pottery and production was resumed under the management of Mr Arthur Cole, who had previously worked at Watcombe. The pottery made during this post-war period consisted mainly of the old favourites of earlier days, including 'Scandy', the 'Black Cockerel', slip-painted daffodils and, possibly, other flowers in pigment colours. The Pottery also revived the production of 'Cottage-and-Motto' slip-ware, the cottages of this period being single-storey buildings with only two windows and a door, rather than the typical two-storey, four-window, Watcombe cottages. But the finish of these later wares, which were distinguished from the 1930s by the presence of the word 'ENGLAND' at the bottom of the mark, is not usually so good as that of the earlier products. As at the parent firm, rising costs and falling demand made it difficult to operate profitably, and in 1957 the Longpark Pottery was finally closed and Mr Cole returned to St. Marychurch to manage the Watcombe factory.

Apart from the kilns, which have since been demolished, the main buildings of the Longpark Works still stand virtually unaltered after enduring nearly a century and a half of alternating activity and neglect (Fig. 123). Even the iron lettering that spells out the words 'LONGPARK POTTERY' still clings to the top of Brunel's Tower as it did in George Easterbrook's time, although the masonry is crumbling and the iron rusty. Only the wholesale greengrocery business now carried on below is different — as different from a Pottery as the Pottery was from a pumping station.

LONGPARK MARKS

(i) *Factory Marks*. Most articles made at Longpark appear to have been marked, although the wares of the Brewer period are seldom recognized owing to the faintness of the scratched marks then used.

41.

Impressed mark found on terra-cotta articles made between 1883 and c.1895. The blank sector is believed originally to have contained the word 'CHINA', but no impression of the unmodified mark has been seen.

42.

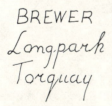

Form of underglaze scratched mark used c.1895−c.1905. The complete mark is rarely visible and sometimes appears to include the word 'England'.

43.

LONGPARK
TORQUAY

Impressed mark used by the Longpark Pottery Co. Ltd., c.1905−c.1910.

157

44 (a)	LONGPARK TORQUAY	Black rubber-stamped mark. c.1910—c.1930.
(b)	LONGPARK TORQUAY DEVON	Circular version of (a), sometimes accompanied by 'ENGLAND'. Seldom seen, probably c.1920.
(c)	TORQUAY LONGPARK	'Inverted' version of (a) only seen on glazed articles with dry bases. c.1922.
45.	TORMOHUN WARE	Impressed mark of the Royal Tormohun Pottery Co. (Art) Ltd., found in association with No. 43. c.1910.
46.	TORMOHUN WARE	Alternative version of No. 45. c.1910.
47 (a)	TORMOHUN LONGPARK TORQUAY	Impressed or rubber-stamped mark of the Royal Tormohun Pottery Co. (Art) Ltd. c.1912.
(b)	TORMOHUN WARE TORQUAY	Alternative version of (a). c.1912.
48.	*Longpark Torquay*	Bold, incised, mark of the Royal Longpark Pottery Co. (Art) Ltd., c.1914—c.1923. The style varies and can be in script or 'lower case' lettering, and up to 100mm in length.

49. *Devon Ware*

Incised mark, similar in style to No. 48, and believed to be an alternative. (N.B. A similar mark was occasionally used by Brannam's Pottery, Barnstaple, at about the same time.)

50. **LONGPARK TORQUAY**

Black, rubber-stamped, mark of the Longpark Pottery Co. Ltd., c.1918—c.1925. The letters are taller in proportion to their width than on the other marks.

51. **LONGPARK TORQUAY ENGLAND**

Black, rubber-stamped, mark: c.1930—1940, and 1947—1957.

(ii) *Pattern Numbers.* Pattern numbers and decoration codes are found incised on glazed wares from c.1895—c.1910. After this period, and until the 1920s, the characters were usually painted in black. Later articles usually have only the factory mark. Longpark had fewer shape numbers than Aller Vale — running to only a few hundreds. Only three decoration codes have been seen, all of Aller Vale type. They are:

N.1: The 'Scandy' pattern, not used much after 1915, originated by Aller Vale.

N.2: The 'Coloured Cockerel' pattern, also done at Aller, and

N.3: The 'Black Cockerel', one of the most popular Longpark patterns. Also done by Watcombe, but not seen on Aller Vale wares.

(iii) *Potters' Marks.* The only craftsman's mark seen on Longpark pottery are the initials 'S.S.' on some articles with oil- or slip-painted decoration. It is possible that these are the initials of a member of the Skinner family.

Section Six

THE SMALLER POTTERIES

There's a joy without canker or cark,
There's a pleasure eternally new,
'Tis to gloat on the glaze and the mark
Of china that's ancient and blue.

Andrew Lang: *Ballade of Blue China.*

Almost from the beginning of the pottery industry in Torquay
there have been a few small firms working in the district, in
addition to the larger factories already described. Until recent
times these were usually the result of a craftsman breaking
away from one of the larger establishments in order to set up
on his own. But in such a cut-throat business, when even the
big factories sometimes found it difficult to keep going, it must
have been even harder for the small concern. Little wonder,
then, that many of them only existed for a few years, before
the proprietor either retired or abandoned the struggle and
went back to Watcombe as an employee.

For obvious reasons these small firms attracted little
publicity in their time, and it is now difficult to obtain detailed
information about their activities. It must not be assumed,
though, that their wares were necessarily inferior to those of
the larger Potteries. Indeed, the reason for their existence was
usually the desire of the proprietor to develop his own ideas
and to make the kind of pottery he liked, rather than be
dictated to by someone else.

163

In this Section will be found, approximately in chronological order, what information it has been possible to collect on all those small potteries that are known to have existed up to the closure of the Watcombe factory, and are now themselves no more. It should also be mentioned that a few new potteries have been established in Torquay since the Second World War, but these are outside the scope of the present book.

6.1. THE KERSWELL ART POTTERY

Amongst the few references to this firm is an entry in the 1889 edition of Kelly's Directory of Devonshire, which indicates that the manager was a Mr J.G. Skinner. Since the address of the Pottery is given as 'Kings Kerswell, Newton Abbot', the Works must have been situated somewhere between the Aller Vale and Longpark Potteries, possibly in a building alongside the main road that subsequently accommodated a steam laundry.

This Mr Skinner was one of the original Watcombe craftsmen, who came from the Staffordshire Potteries with Mr Brock, and was the father of Mr R.H. Skinner who ran the Longpark Pottery in the 'twenties and 'thirties of the present century. Like several of the other Watcombe men, Mr J.G. Skinner probably left that firm at the time when it closed down between 1883 and 1884 and set up a Pottery of his own.

The only example of the work of this firm encountered so far is the small, slip-cast, terracotta bust of Joseph Chamberlain illustrated in Fig. 124. Apart from the old-style inscription 'Published by the Kerswell Art Pottery, Kings Kerswell, South Devon' scratched on the back, this piece has 'J.G.S. '87' moulded on one side, suggesting that the original was modelled by Mr Skinner himself. This tends to confirm the belief that Mr Skinner had been a modeller at Watcombe and that he was capable of original work.

It is not known what other types of terracotta were made by the Kerswell Art Pottery. Undoubtedly, there would have been

165

a range of busts and figures, and probably ornamental vases similar to the Watcombe products of the 'eighties. The firm is not mentioned in later editions of the local directory, and it probably did not operate for more than a decade or so.

6.2. THE BROOMHILL POTTERY

The 1889 and 1893 editions of Kelly's Directory list a Henry Brewer as a terracotta manufacturer at 'Broomhill, St. Mary Church, Torquay'. Mr Brewer was another member of the original team of Staffordshire potters at the Watcombe Works who decided (or was obliged) to set up on his own in the mid-'eighties. He operated at the back of a row of terraced houses on the north side of the Hele Road, midway between Lowe's Bridge and Hele Cross. These houses still stand with their original name of 'Broomhill Cottages', but there now seems to be no trace of the Pottery.

Mr Brewer had also been employed at Watcombe as a modeller, and it seems likely that at Broomhill he originally made terracotta wares decorated with oil painting. However, no examples of this class of work have been seen with a mark that can be attributed to this Pottery and the firm is known only for glazed, slip-decorated, red earthenwares of Aller Vale type. These were scratch-marked, usually very faintly: 'Brewer/Barton/Torquay', and should not be confused with the wares of *the* Barton Pottery which operated in the twentieth century.

Examples of Broomhill glazed pottery are fairly common, although seldom recognized. The style of decoration most frequently encountered consists of Aller Vale type coloured scrolls on a dark green ground together with a motto scratched through a band of cream-coloured slip — a combination never found on genuine Aller Vale wares. A typical example of this pattern can be seen on the small vase shown in Fig. 125. The colours are quite distinctive and enable this type of pottery, when once seen, to be identified on sight. Other types of decoration included slip-painted flowers on cream or green grounds, but the quality of the ware was very variable.

The Broomhill Pottery was mainly a family business, with Mr Brewer's two sons, William and James, helping their father. William had also worked at Watcombe (as a turner) and both sons subsequently went into partnership with a Mr Willott to run the Longpark Pottery. Henry Brewer presumably retired towards the end of the nineteenth century.

6.3. BREWER BROTHERS & LAMY

After giving up the Longpark Pottery in 1905, William and James Brewer moved to St. Marychurch itself and commenced the manufacture of pottery at the rear of their house in Park Road. They were associated in this venture with a French artist named Lamy,* which suggests that their wares were competently decorated. No pottery attributable to this business has been identified. The partnership, if such it was, came to an end about the time of the Great War, and William Brewer then returned to work at Watcombe.

*The only known artist of this name is the P.F. Lamy who exhibited a painting with the title 'Printemps fleuri' at the Paris Salon of 1891.

6.4. THE TOR VALE ART POTTERY

This little-known Pottery is mentioned only in the 1913—14 and 1923—24 editions of the Torquay Times' Directory of Torquay, which give its address as '43, Teignmouth Road'. The name of the business, which is believed to have existed until the late nineteen-twenties, was taken from the small road called Tor Vale which leads off the Teignmouth Road in the Torre district of Torquay.

Only one marked example of the work of this firm has been encountered — a vase of nondescript shape made from a warm brown clay containing small white particles, similar to the usual Hart and Moist body. This is decorated in underglaze pigment colours, on a white ground, with a crude pattern of bright red and green patches separated by irregular black lines, rather like a leaded glass window. Since this design bears some resemblance to the 'jazz' patterns produced by the larger Torquay firms in the 'twenties, it seems probable that the Tor Vale Pottery also imitated other contemporary styles of decoration. Indeed, this firm may have been the source of a range of vases, teapots, and other articles painted with a very poor version of the 'Kingfisher' pattern that were rubber-stamped only with the mark 'TORQUAY' or 'Made in England'. A distinctive feature of these wares is the peculiar salmon-pink colour of the glazed body where it is not concealed by the blue ground.

171

6.5. THE DAISON POTTERY

Lemon and Crute

The Daison Pottery was started just after the Great War by Mr H.E. Crute, in partnership with a Mr Tom (?) Lemon, and was situated on the Teignmouth Road at the corner of Trumlands Road. The original name of the firm, as recorded in the 1923 edition of Kelly's Directory, was simply 'Lemon and Crute'. Harry Crute was well known as a decorator in the Torquay potteries and had worked for Mr Staddon at Hele Cross before, and perhaps during, the War (see Fig. 56). Earlier still, he is believed to have been at Watcombe. Little is known for certain about Mr Lemon. He was possibly a member of the family of that name which ran the Weston-super-Mare Pottery, although he originally came to Torquay from one of the Barnstaple potteries. There are also grounds for believing that he may have spent some years about the time of the War running the Art side of the Longpark Pottery.

The Daison Pottery took its name from the near-by Daison estate, a place of considerable antiquity, originally spelt 'Dazon'. The Works themselves occupied a comparatively small site, that could hardly have provided room for more than half a dozen workpeople. Yet, despite this, the firm managed to operate two small kilns on an alternate firing and loading cycle.

The wares produced at the Daison Pottery in the early

173

'twenties consisted mainly of hand-thrown articles decorated underglaze with pigment colours. As might be expected of a firm whose proprietors were decorators, the quality of the painting was generally superior to much of the rather crude decoration done by firms such as the Longpark and Torquay potteries.

One of the most popular of the early styles of decoration consisted of butterflies, birds or flowers painted on a streaky mauve-pink ground. The butterflies are much softer in outline than those done at Longpark about the same time, the broken texture giving the impression of a crayon drawing on rough paper. Amongst the flower subjects painted on the same streaky ground the most common was a spray of white heather with a fern leaf in the foreground. It should be noted, however, that this pattern is also found, but with a lilac ground, on Watcombe pottery of the 'thirties. Articles decorated with these standard patterns included vases, tea-services, mugs, beakers, and condiment sets, together with a type of footed bowl with three skewed handles that is typical of Daison (Fig. 126). Alternatively, a combination of slip and pigment colours was sometimes used in a decorative scheme, as in the case of the cream jug and sugar bowl shown in Fig. 127.

Another range of wares with simple curved shapes, such as bottle-vases, shallow bowls, and plant pots, was also made in the mid-'twenties and decorated with flown glazes, usually in subdued shades of blue and green. Although many of these were formed on the wheel others were evidently slip-cast, for, long after the Pottery had closed down, a number of old plaster moulds were found on the site.

Unlike the larger Torquay firms, the Daison Pottery had no clay pit of its own and had to buy supplies wherever it could. Visitors who asked Harry Crute where he obtained his clay were often shocked by the unexpected reply: "Oh, I've often had a load from the cemetery when they've been digging a grave"! For this reason the body colour of Daison pottery is somewhat variable, although it is usually of the light or medium red colour associated with the Watcombe and Hele Cross Potteries.

A characteristic feature of Daison pottery of the early 'twenties is the dry, unglazed, base showing horse-shoe lines where the article was cut from the wheel with a wire loop. The usual mark on such ware was 'Lemon & Crute/Torquay' incised with a sharp point, sometimes accompanied by a two- or three-figure pattern number done with a much blunter tool.* However, many of these dry-base pieces are marked only with a pattern number, while others have no mark at all. By the mid-'twenties it became usual to glaze the bases of articles and these were given a rubber-stamped Pottery mark with the same words arranged in a semi-circle. After this change pattern numbers were not normally marked on the wares.

The Daison Birds

From about 1925 the streaky pink was abandoned in favour of a uniform blue as the most popular ground colour for hand-painted wares, in accordance with the general Torquay style of the period. One shade, typical of this Pottery, was a pale powder-blue; the other was a vivid sky-blue which is only found, elsewhere, on early Barton wares. Articles decorated on these grounds were usually finished with the black rims so fashionable at the time.

Surprisingly, in a seaside resort, Mr Crute is credited with having been the first Torquay decorator to use sea-gulls as a motif,** and many small Daison pieces were painted with one or more gulls, done in black and white with yellow feet above white-crested waves on the pale blue ground (Fig. 127). Although these souvenirs must have been produced by the hundreds the painting is comparatively detailed, and an enthusiastic admirer of Mr Crute's work once remarked: "Harry's sea-gulls are *real* birds, you can even see the feathers!"

Birds, in fact, seem to have been the favourite decorative subject on Daison wares of this period. Most of the Torquay potteries were then producing articles painted with kingfishers on a blue ground, and the Daison Pottery was no exception. Some people in Torquay maintain that it was Harry Crute who

*The only other Torquay firm at this time which produced glazed wares with a dry base was the Longpark Pottery.

**This distinction has also been claimed for the Barton Pottery.

originated the 'Kingfisher' pattern, rather than Mr Hunt of Watcombe. But whatever the relative merits of the rival claims to the subject, some of the Daison versions do little to support the artistic reputations of the firm's proprietors and were probably painted by assistants.

Since other birds painted at Daison included peacocks, Mr Crute was evidently less superstitious than his former employer at Hele Cross, Mr Staddon. However, as far as is known, mottoes were never incorporated on articles made at this Pottery — presumably because they were thought to be in bad taste! Another style of decoration occasionally found on Daison wares showed pixies dancing on toadstools; a recurrent, if rare, subject with several of the Torquay potteries.

A small pottery such as Daison had to select its 'lines' very carefully if it were to avoid bankruptcy by producing articles that were too good for the market. It is therefore surprising to find that the firm turned out a small number of pieces that were far superior to the run-of-the-mill tourist wares — much better, in fact, than anything produced by the other Torquay potteries at that time. As one example of this better-quality work, Fig. 128 shows a pair of vases decorated, probably by Mr Crute himself, with blue-tits on the powder-blue ground. Although the style of decoration is much simpler than that of the late-Victorian bird subjects done at Watcombe the general effect, for what must have been a repetition pattern, is very pleasing. It is also interesting to note the two small skewed handles of characteristic Barnstaple form, for which Mr Lemon was presumably responsible.

About 1928 Mr Lemon withdrew from the partnership and went to a pottery near Bournemouth, taking one of the throwers with him. Mr. Crute was then joined by Mr Barker, one of the Watcombe decorators, and re-formed the business as 'H.E. Crute & Co. (Torquay) Ltd.', trading as the 'Daison Art Pottery'. After the reorganization the firm continued to use a semi-circular rubber-stamped mark, but with the words 'Daison Art Pottery' substituted for 'Lemon & Crute'.

Another very competent decorator associated with the Daison Pottery was Henry Birbeck (always known as 'Harry'), the son of the Holland Birbeck who decorated for both the Watcombe Pottery and the Torquay Terra-Cotta Company in the nineteenth century. Harry Birbeck had also worked at the Watcombe and Torquay Potteries (see Fig. 56) and probably joined Harry Crute's firm in the 1920s. His painting retained much of the meticulous attention to detail of his father's style, and a fine Daison vase decorated by him with a mallard rising from reed-fringed water is illustrated in Fig. 130. The painting is done in a subdued range of greys and greens with contrasting touches of brighter colours on the bird's feathers, the general effect being reminiscent more of the contemporary china vases produced by Doulton's at Burslem than typical Torquay pottery. Another unusual feature of this piece, for Torquay ware, is that it is signed on the outside by the artist.

The Daison Pottery did not long survive Mr Lemon's departure, although there is some doubt as to when it actually closed down. The last Directory entry occurs in Kelly's 1931 edition, and the firm is not mentioned in the 1933 edition or subsequently. It seems, therefore, that H.E. Crute & Co. (Torquay) Ltd. failed to weather the depression of the 'thirties and went into liquidation some years before the Second World War. Mr Crute is known then to have returned to the Watcombe Pottery as a decorator, and subsequently acted as a traveller for that firm. Later still, about 1960, he is understood to have been associated with the Dartmouth Pottery.

The buildings of the Daison Pottery remained unoccupied until after the War, when the kilns were demolished during the course of road-widening operations. Since the late 'sixties the remainder of the site has been occupied as a car-breaker's yard.

M

6.6. THE BARTON POTTERY

The business generally known as the Barton Pottery was apparently established in 1922 as the Mayville Pottery by a group of five men trading as H.F. Jackson and Company. Apart from Mr Harry Jackson this partnership (as it then appears to have been) included a Mr Ellis Sidney Forster, who had previously worked at the Watcombe Pottery and originally hailed from Staffordshire, Mr John Bradford, Mr Alfred Macey, and a Mr Alexander Hudson. Mr Bradford, who was the thrower, was presumably a member of the family of that name who had worked at the Aller Vale Pottery, but the backgrounds of the other partners are not known.

The Pottery was set up in buildings at the corner of the Barton Road and Audley Avenue which had formerly been occupied by a monumental mason. The premises already included a yard surrounded on three sides by workshops, and to these a single kiln was added. The existing showroom facing the Barton Road continued to serve the same purpose for the new business while Mr Forster, who appears to have acted as the manager, occupied the adjacent house.

No reference to the Mayville Pottery, under this name, has been found in the local Directories, and the firm is not mentioned in Kelly's Directory until the 1926 edition, where it appears as 'Barton Potteries Ltd.' From this, and the fact that no ware has been seen with the word Mayville included in the mark, it would seem that the original partnership was of short duration and that the business must have been reconstituted as

179

a Limited Company soon after it was started. This reorganization confirmed Mr Forster as the head of the firm, for he is always referred to locally as the Managing Director of the Barton Pottery during the remainder of its existence.

If Daison was a decorator's Pottery, then Barton must be known for its colours and glazes, for Mr Forster was regarded as an expert in this branch of ceramics. Certainly, all the Barton wares have a very fine glaze, while the colours are generally clean and bright. Like Mr Crute at the Daison Pottery, Mr Forster produced a great variety of articles, mostly of small to medium size and intended for the tourist trade. Although some early wares were decorated on a white ground the distinctive feature of much Barton pottery is a vivid sky-blue ground, brighter than the typical Daison blue but not so dark as the blues used by the other Torquay potteries. The Barton Pottery was also like Daison in that it had no clay pit of its own and had to buy clay wherever it could. There was probably no difficulty with supplies, as the Works were close to the Torquay (Hele Cross) and Longpark Potteries and almost opposite the cemetery, within which lies some of the best red clay. However, the variable colour and quality of the firm's basic raw material resulted in a corresponding range of body colour in the finished wares, from light red to dark brown.

Some of the earliest Barton pottery consisted of spill vases decorated with red roses on a black trellis, painted in pigment colours over a white ground and closely resembling the Watcombe vase shown in Fig. 31. Like all the firm's later wares these have a circular rubber-stamped mark incorporating the words 'Barton Pottery Ltd./Torquay'. Mr Forster, or rather his decorators, also share with Mr Crute the reputation of having been the first persons to depict sea-gulls on Torquay pottery. But there is no difficulty in distinguishing the two types of bird, for the Daison gulls were painted in pigments and shown on the wing, while the Barton version is done in slip and stands stolidly on a brown rock, like the sea-gull in the Torquay coat of arms (Fig. 129). Other blue-ground articles, such as cream jugs, were left without any further decoration, except perhaps a black rim or handle.

Moonlight scenes were another Barton speciality, for which a darker blue ground was very appropriate. For standard lines the painting on these was often both competent and effective, even if the shapes of some of the vases were rather ugly. Fig. 131, for example, shows a large vase decorated with a cottage in moonlight; the building and surrounding trees being done mainly in black and white, but with small touches of red firelight showing through the windows. Fishing boats were also painted in the same style — an interesting variation of the daytime and evening representations that were done by the other Torquay potteries.

Yet another, completely different, type of decoration on Barton pottery is that of the jam pot shown in Fig. 129. Here the outside of the article has been dipped in white slip on which very wet pigment colours, chiefly blue and red, have been splashed almost like coloured inks. As with all the Barton wares, this pot is finished with the clear lustrous glaze for which the firm was noted.

For the first few years of its existence the Barton Pottery appears to have been successful, and charabanc parties queued up on the footpath outside the showroom for conducted tours of the Works. Mr Forster was very popular with his colleagues and staff of about a dozen, and is said to have been 'a wonderful man to work with'. Despite this the Barton Pottery acquired the reputation of being an unlucky place and by the early 'thirties it seems to have been in financial difficulties. According to local opinion this was because Mr Forster spent too much time ensuring the technical perfection of his wares. However, the real reason was more probably the trade depression of the period, which resulted in even the large firms, like Watcombe, having to lay off many of their workpeople. With a larger business than Mr Crute, Mr Forster was able to hold out for longer than the Daison Pottery, although he was obliged to reorganize the firm, probably with additional financial support, as 'Barton Potteries (1934) Ltd.' Unfortunately, this action failed to save the business and it is not mentioned in the local Directories after 1935. From this it is concluded that the Barton Pottery closed down just before the Second World War.

Although the kiln has now been demolished, the buildings of the Barton Pottery still stand much as they did in the 'twenties, and when last seen were occupied by an office cleaning firm.

MARKS OF THE SMALLER TORQUAY POTTERIES

THE KERSWELL ART POTTERY

Only two examples (busts) of the work of this firm have been seen. These had the following incised mark (c.1887 +):

52.   Published by the "Kerswell Art Pottery",
                     Kings Kerswell,
                     South Devon.

THE BREWER (BROOMHILL) POTTERY

53.   BREWER   Incised mark found on glazed
        Barton   wares. c.1885 — c.1895.
        Torquay

THE DAISON POTTERY

(i) *Factory Marks.* Early wares are sometimes unmarked. Later wares usually have a rubber-stamped mark.

54 (a)

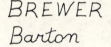

Lemon & Crute
Torquay

                            Incised mark on articles with
                            an unglazed base. c.1922 —
                            c.1925.

(b)	*Lole*	Abbreviated form of (a), found on small articles.
55.	LEMON & CRUTE TORQUAY	Black, rubber-stamped, under-glaze mark. c.1925—c.1928.
56.	DAISON ART POTTERY TORQUAY	Black, rubber-stamped, under-glaze mark. c.1928—c.1932.

(ii) *Pattern Numbers.* Early wares often have a pattern number of up to three figures incised on the dry base. This number probably relates to the shape, rather than the decoration, and is scored much more heavily than the factory mark.

57.	*161*	Typical Daison pattern number. The bar indicates that the figures are to be read this way up.

In the absence of a factory mark a number of this type, on a dry base, indicates a Daison provenance.

(iii) *Decorators' Marks.* Decorators included Harry Crute, Henry ('Harry') Birbeck, and a Mr Hunt. Only one signed article has been seen: a vase with 'H. Birbeck' painted on the side.

THE BARTON POTTERY

(i) *Factory Mark.*

58.	 BARTON POTTERY TORQUAY LTD	This black, rubber-stamped, underglaze mark appears to have been applied to all Barton wares throughout the Pottery's existence. c.1922—c.1936.

(ii) *Pattern Numbers.* No pattern numbers have been found on Barton pottery, but one rubber-stamped Registered Design Number has been seen associated with Mark No. 58.

THE TOR VALE POTTERY

59.

Tor Vale

49

Painted mark, in black, with pattern number. c.1923.

Section Seven

OTHER TORQUAY-TYPE POTTERIES

Fig. iv.   Drawing of an example of traditional Scandinavian 'rosemaling' (rose-painting). It is believed that the decorative slip patterns originally used by the Exeter and Hart & Moist Art potteries (see Fig. 133) were based on this style of painting, which came to be known locally as 'Scandy'.

   The well-known 'Scandy' pattern of the Aller Vale Pottery was a particular version of this type of decoration based on an 'Old Rhodian' (Isnik) design.

Who *is* the Potter, pray, and who the Pot?

Fitzgerald: *Omar Khayyam*.

In addition to the potteries on the northern outskirts of Torquay several other firms, rather further afield, were producing Torquay-type wares during the first half of the present century. By 'Torquay-type' ware is meant pottery having all, or most, of the characteristics typical of pottery made in Torquay itself at that time; i.e. a red or brown body decorated with standard patterns painted in coloured slips (or pigments) on a slip-coated ground, sometimes with scratched mottoes, and finished with a clear glaze. Since such wares can easily be mistaken for actual Torquay pottery, especially if unmarked, brief descriptions of some of these 'out-potteries' have been included in this Section for completeness.

7.1. THE EXETER ART POTTERY

During the last decade of the nineteenth century a small Pottery was established in a former malt-house at 7, Exe Street, Exeter, by two partners named Cole and Trelease. The business, which was known as the 'Exeter Art Pottery', existed only from 1892 to 1896. Little information is available as to the nature of the wares produced although, from the use of the word 'Art' in the name, it may be assumed that they were intended to be mainly ornamental.

All the articles seen bearing this firm's mark have been mugs and jugs, of almost archaic appearance, heavily potted in brown clay. These are usually dipped in white slip on the outside and finished with an amber glaze, although khaki and blue grounds are also found. A typical shape is a straight-sided mug with two thick handles, the decoration often consisting of a heavily-scratched inscription, sometimes accompanied by a fictitiously early date, e.g. '1692'. A characteristic feature of these mugs, of which examples are shown in Fig. 132, is the way the handles are cut off square at the lower end.

The Exeter Art Pottery is sometimes confused with Hart and Moist's Devon Art Pottery. However, there should be no difficulty in distinguishing the products of the two firms (when marked) for Cole and Trelease used distinctive impressed marks formed from the words 'Exeter Art Pottery' disposed in either a circular or semi-circular arrangement.

191

7.2. HART AND MOIST

The largest manufacturer of Torquay-type wares outside Torquay itself was the Hart and Moist Pottery in Exeter. This business was started in 1894 by a Mr Alfred Moist, in partnership with a Mr William Hart, in Bonhay Road, down by the river. Mr Moist did the potting while Mr Hart, who had previously worked for Cole and Trelease, was the fireman or 'kiln-burner'. Some time about the beginning of the present century the Works were transferred to a site just below Exe Bridge, and the address was then given as: Haven Road, St. Thomas's. Mr Alfred Moist was later joined by his younger brother Joseph, who is said to have served his apprenticeship with a pottery in the North of England.

At the beginning of this century the Hart and Moist business was known as the 'Devon Art Pottery'. Subsequently, in Edwardian times, the prefix 'Royal' was added after the firm had received the patronage of Queen Alexandra. Unfortunately, the description 'Devon Art Pottery' was also used by a Mr Alexander Lauder at his pottery in Barnstaple about the same time and there is, therefore, some risk of confusing the two firms. However, Lauder's appear to have applied this description to their wares, rather than to their factory, whereas the reverse was the case at Exeter.

Considering the proximity of the two firms, it is not surprising that the earliest Hart and Moist wares were very similar to those of the short-lived Exeter Art Pottery. Indeed, it seems probable that when the latter closed down in 1896 some

193

of the other craftsmen may have gone to work for Hart and Moist. If the number of articles that have survived bears any relation to the number produced then the output of the Bonhay Road Pottery consisted mainly of useful wares, such as mugs, jugs and plates. These were usually finished with a white slip exterior and decorated, under an amber glaze, with patterns done in coloured slips together with scratched mottoes or verses (Fig. 133). Like the wares of the Exeter Art Pottery, the early Hart and Moist articles often look much older than they are and, although they are generally less clumsy, the lettering is often poorly done and in backward-sloping characters. Another feature of the mugs of this type is the neatly turned and recessed base and the russet brown colour of the glazed interior.

The decorative motifs on the amber-glazed wares ranged from a simple two-lobed 'wings' device, resembling an owl in flight, to quite elaborate scroll patterns. Some of these designs have a certain resemblance to the traditional Norwegian style of decoration known as 'rosemaling' (rose-painting) as can be seen by comparing the example shown in Fig. 133 with Fig. iv. It may therefore be that this was the type of decoration originally described as Scandinavian, and that the description was subsequently abbreviated to 'Scandy' and applied to the characteristic Aller Vale pattern.

The colours of these early Hart and Moist patterns were mostly restricted to a blue-grey (which often appears green under the yellow glaze) and terracotta, together with a little white. Unfortunately, few of the articles are clearly marked, although the Exeter Museum has a marked plate that was made to commemorate the election of the first Mayor of Greater Exeter in 1900.

The same blue slip was also used as the ground colour for a characteristically shaped two-handled tankard, much taller than the average Hart and Moist mug and usually decorated with the 'wings' motif and a long inscription (Fig. 133). Unlike the amber-glazed wares these tankards have only been seen with a thin, semi-matt, glaze, and the ground colour is occasionally khaki instead of blue. In the absence of a mark examples are sometimes wrongly identified as Barnstaple ware, but it should be noted that similar articles were previously made at both the Exeter Art Pottery and Aller Vale and these were usually marked.

Imitation Aller Vale Wares

It was not long, however, before Hart and Moist abandoned these early styles of pottery and began to specialize in slip-decorated wares that were passable imitations of most of the Aller Vale patterns. Fig. 135 shows several typical examples made during the early nineteen-hundreds. They include a waisted vase with skewed handles that is decorated with a polychrome scroll design on a dark green ground, a coffee pot with 'Scandy'-type decoration, and a globular pot with white scrolls on a blue ground. All these articles are impressed 'H.M. Exeter', which was the firm's usual mark in Edwardian times. Hart and Moist also copied the Aller Vale 'Sandringham' pattern of blue scrolls on a white ground, while the ornamental jug of Fig. 134 seems to be after the Aller B.4 pattern* (see Fig. 85).

This plagiarism is not entirely surprising, for William Hart is believed to have worked at the Aller Vale Pottery in his younger days. In fact, it is possible that the Exeter firm engaged decorators from Aller Vale when the latter was being run down in favour of Watcombe during the years preceding the Great War. It would have been only natural in the circumstances for these craftsmen to have gone on producing what were, by then, traditional patterns. However, it is interesting to note that the central motif of Hart and Moist's version of the 'Scandy' design usually (but not invariably) consists of a leaf shape with a sharp central point, in contrast to the three or five 'feathers' with rounded tips that are characteristic of genuine Torquay 'Scandy'.

All Hart and Moist pottery has a speckled brown, or reddish-brown, body — more like some of the Longpark clay than the finer stuff used at Aller and Watcombe — which was obtained locally. The firm never seems to have worked in white

*Although other Torquay potteries had no compunction about marking their versions of Aller Vale patterns with the original decoration codes, no pattern numbers or codes have been seen on Hart and Moist pottery.

clay as a body material and used whatever manufacturing process was most appropriate to each kind of product. The smaller and symmetrical mugs, vases, and bowls were evidently hand-thrown, while articles of irregular shape, such as the jug of Fig. 134, were produced by moulding or slip-casting. This rather ugly object, which has the oval cross-section popular for cottage ornaments in Edwardian times, is covered in a dark green slip with the moulded, raised, design picked out in cream and yellow.

Mr Alfred Moist died in 1910, and Mr Hart retired in 1921, leaving Mr Joseph Moist as sole proprietor. At this time the Royal Devon Art Pottery was evidently still a thriving concern. Its wares were sold locally to tourists at Worth's (the art dealers in Cathedral Close) as well as being distributed to other parts of the country. The proximity of the Works to the wharves of the Exeter Canal also enabled the firm to build up a considerable export trade to the Continent.

According to an advertisement in the *Pottery Gazette* in 1915, Hart and Moist claimed to produce 'Art Pottery in all shapes, colours and designs', and indicated that 'Mottoed Wares' were a speciality. From other notices it appears that the mottoes were chiefly in dialect, the sugar basin of Fig. 135 being inscribed 'Help yersel tae sugar'. It should be mentioned, though, that the finish of many of the firm's products was decidedly inferior to that of most contemporary Torquay pottery.

Despite its earlier prosperity, the Royal Devon Art Pottery closed down in the mid-'thirties, presumably as a result of the trade depression at that time. The last mention of the firm in Bezely's Exeter Directory occurs in the 1935 edition; although Mr Joseph Moist survived until January 1954, when the *Express and Echo* reported his death at the age of eighty-two. The Pottery buildings were badly damaged by bombs during the Second World War, and have since been demolished.

7.3. THE BOVEY TRACEY POTTERIES

The manufacture of pottery at Bovey Tracey, some ten miles north of Torquay, is of very ancient origin. As mentioned in the Introduction, the Teign valley abounds with beds of white clay and the existence of outcrops of lignite (soft coal) had led to the establishment of one or two small potteries near Bovey by the middle of the eighteenth century. In 1790 the great Josiah Wedgwood visited the district, while investigating possible sources of material for his Staffordshire factory, and noted that 'the clay was good but the coal poor'.

The original potteries eventually closed down as the lignite was used up, but in 1842 one of the old Works was enlarged and reopened as 'The Bovey Tracey Pottery Company' by a Captain Buller and a Mr Divett. After the construction of a branch railway line past the works the firm was able to obtain hard coal from Somerset, and in this way developed into a flourishing business, comparable in size with one of the larger Staffordshire factories.

During the nineteenth century the Bovey Tracey Pottery specialized in the manufacture of white earthenware, of medium quality, of the kind usually associated with the Staffordshire Potteries. The Bovey tablewares were generally decorated with blue transfer-printing and were supplied to the West of England market as well as being exported to Mediterranean countries. The firm also had large contracts with the Admiralty for supplying the Navy. Following a change of ownership in the eighteen-nineties the business was re-formed as 'The Bovey Pottery Co. Ltd.'; but this did not affect the nature of its wares, and the firm continued to operate under the new name for the remainder of its existence.

The Bovey Tracey Art Pottery

About 1908 a Mr Enoch Staddon, who had previously worked at the Bovey Pottery, took over the Works at Hele Cross, on the outskirts of Torquay, which had formerly been operated by the Torquay Terra-Cotta Company. The Torquay Pottery, as Mr Staddon called the Hele Cross Works, was a red-clay Pottery that specialized in souvenir-type wares for the tourist trade. It was evidently a profitable business in its early years, for just after the Great War Mr Staddon acquired a plot of ground opposite the Bovey Pottery to establish a second Works, which he called 'The Bovey Tracey Art Pottery'. This consisted of a single low building equipped with a small muffle-type kiln, and was fitted out to produce ornamental pottery of the same general type as the Torquay Pottery.

Mr Staddon's reason for starting a second business on the doorstep of his old firm was probably the knowledge that he could persuade his friends at the Bovey Pottery to cross the road to work for him, when they would have been unwilling to move to Torquay.

The articles made at the Bovey Art Pottery, as it was known locally, were usually thrown from a red or reddish-brown clay and decorated with coloured slips and pigments in the contemporary Torquay style. One of the earliest examples of the firm's work is the bowl illustrated in Fig. 136. This is interesting for two reasons. Not only is it signed and dated underneath: '"Gertie" Summerfield, Bovey Tracey 19-10-22', but it is decorated, on a cream ground, with a version of the 'Kingfisher' design that later became so popular at Longpark and other Torquay potteries. Since the decoration has all the features of the fully-developed 'Kingfisher' pattern, except an all-over blue ground, this bowl provides useful evidence, not only that this pattern must have been evolved soon after the Great War, but that the blue ground did not become general until a year or so after 1922. Since the only other potteries known to have painted the 'Kingfisher' on a cream ground were Aller Vale (which closed down in 1924) and Mr Staddon's other factory at Hele Cross, it seems possible that it was one of his decorators who introduced the design to the Torquay potteries. If so, it is surprising that Mr Staddon did not make more articles decorated in this way during the late 'twenties and 'thirties.

Another article from the Bovey Art Pottery with distinctive shape and type of decoration is the 'Egyptian' style vase of Fig. 137, which was probably inspired by the discovery of Tutankhamun's tomb in the early twenties. This has a spiral groove turned into its surface to imitate the coiled construction of ancient pottery, and is finished with a thin wash of glazed black pigment below a border of irregular stripes of bright enamel colours.

That Mr Staddon's two potteries were regarded simply as two branches of a single business is shown by the fact that many of the shapes and decorative patterns were common to both Works. Fig. 68, for example, illustrates two bowls of similar size and shape; one decorated with a typical Hele Cross butterfly on a plain blue ground and marked 'TORQUAY/POTTERY/ENGLAND', the other painted with a green and orange leaf design on a mottled blue ground and marked 'BOVEY TRACEY/ART POTTERY/DEVON'. The third article in the group is a vase decorated with the same leaf pattern but marked 'ROYAL/TORQUAY/POTTERY/ENGLAND'. Like most twentieth-century Torquay pottery all these pieces have flat, glazed, bases and were fired on stilts.

The Bovey Art Pottery was never a very large concern and did not attain the size or quality of workmanship of the Torquay Pottery at its best. During its later years, at least, it was managed by a Mr Vincent Kane, who was Mr Staddon's son-in-law and had previously worked at the Torquay Pottery (see Fig. 56). However, like the Hele Cross Works, the Bovey Art Pottery had to close down during the Second World War. After Mr Staddon's retirement during the War the site passed into other hands and the buildings are now occupied by Devonshire Potteries Ltd. for the production of slip-cast ornaments made of white clay.

The Devon Tors Pottery

In 1921 another small Pottery was established within a few yards of Mr Staddon's Bovey Art Pottery. The new firm was called the 'Devon Tors Pottery' and was set up by four employees of the Bovey Pottery: William and Frank Bond, Robert Fry, and Ernest Wyatt. In the early days these men continued to work for the large firm during normal hours, and then crossed the road to run their own business in their spare time! After a few years, though, they were able to break away from the Bovey Pottery and develop the Devon Tors as a full-time activity.

The Devon Tors Pottery produced mainly small souvenir-type wares, such as mugs, jugs, beakers, vases and teapots. These were hand-thrown from a fine, pale red, clay and usually had an unglazed base with the words 'DEVON/TORS/POTTERY' impressed in small capital letters. The clay, which was obtained from Torquay (possibly from Mr Staddon's site), was originally prepared by the old Aller method of running slip down a heated fluke until it was firm enough to be cut out at the other end. It was then wedged before use without going through a pugging stage. Later, about 1950, the firm acquired a clay press.

The Pottery employed all the usual decorating techniques, such as slip and pigment painting and sgraffito work. Although some of their patterns were original many of the others, like the 'Scandy' and 'Cottage' designs, were copies of popular Torquay motifs. The firm also copied the Egyptian style of decoration introduced by the Bovey Art Pottery next door.

One example of an original style of Devon Tors work is the small beaker of Fig. 138. This is decorated with a scratched representation of 'Bill Brewer' of the *Widecombe Fair* ballad, looking rather like Bruce Bairnsfather's 'Old Bill' of the 1914—18 War. An interesting characteristic of this beaker is the way the cream-coloured slip has been scraped away progressively to give a suggestion of shading to the man's hair.

From the late 'twenties the firm took to glazing the bases of its wares, in the usual Torquay manner. Such wares, when they were marked, were sometimes rubber-stamped with the letters 'D.T.' inside a diamond, but other articles can be found with only an impressed capital 'B' (for 'Bovey'). By this time the firm was making some quite large pieces, including jardinieres of up to nine or ten inches in diameter. These can be found decorated with a version of the 'Kingfisher' pattern on a bright blue ground, but with the birds in low relief in the style of the 'Parrot' vases of the Torquay Pottery. However, like much of the painting done at Devon Tors, the painting is often garish and rather naïve.

One of the main 'lines' at the Devon Tors Pottery was always the production of small glazed earthenware bottles to contain 'Devon Violets' and other scents produced in the county. These were made by several of the Torquay potteries, including Mr Staddon's two factories, and were typically decorated with a spray of violets painted on a white ground, together with a description of their contents scratched through the slip (Fig. 71). The principal customer for these bottles was Aidees of Torquay, and about 1970 an arrangement was made whereby Aidees took over and demolished the old Pottery buildings and erected a factory and offices on the site for the production of their range of perfumery. However, the manufacture of pottery has not ceased entirely, for Mr Kenneth Bond, a son of one of the original partners, is still engaged in making scent containers and pomanders within the new building.

* * *

At the main Bovey Pottery production of white earthenware continued after the Second World War, and the firm turned out large numbers of mugs to commemorate the coronation of Queen Elizabeth II. Nevertheless, the business was becoming increasingly unprofitable and, after a protracted strike in 1957, the proprietors decided to close the factory. The *Western Morning News* noted in November of the following year that the 'high conical kilns' were then being demolished, and the remaining extensive buildings are now used by an agricultural firm. Fortunately, a few of the smaller kilns escaped destruction and are now the only surviving examples of what was once a common feature of the district (Fig. 139).

7.4. THE CROWN DORSET POTTERY

Away from South Devon the most obvious place for the manufacture of Torquay-type pottery was Barnstaple, in the north of the county. Here three firms: Brannam, Baron, and Lauder were producing red-clay wares up to the time of the Great War.* But these potteries tended to concentrate on the local type of sgraffito decoration in combination with coloured glazes and, apart from some mugs with fairly long inscriptions (usually in verse), avoided the worst trivialities of the South Devon factories.

The combination of coloured clay and a well-developed tourist trade, the essential prerequisites for a successful business in Torquay-type wares, did, however, exist in the adjoining county of Dorset. The region surrounding Poole Harbour has been a source of clay since pre-historic times, and several potteries were working in the district during the nineteenth century. The best known of these, now called the Poole Pottery, is noted for its white-bodied wares, although it did produce some ornamental earthenware with a brown body in the early years of the present century. The local brown clay was also used by a Pottery in Green Road, near the Quay and Gas Works, that is believed to have been started about 1900 by a Charles Collard who had served his apprenticeship at the Aller Vale Pottery. This factory was known as the 'Crown Dorset Pottery', although it was also referred to locally as the

*C.H. Brannam Ltd. is, of course, still in active operation.

203

'Poole Art Pottery'. The firm won several Gold Medals for its wares in the years before the Great War and, from a mug made to commemorate the coronation of King George V and Queen Mary in 1911, it is evident that the Pottery employed the same mixture of decorative techniques as did the Torquay potteries at that time. However, the type of pottery most likely to be confused with Torquay was the range of 'Devon Wares' which were made in the early 'twenties after Mr Collard had left for the Honiton Pottery in 1918.

These articles, which are encountered about as frequently (or infrequently) as Hart and Moist pottery, were made from a uniform brown clay that has none of the red tinge of most of the Torquay bodies. Examples noted have all been fairly small, from three to six inches in height, and are usually decorated underglaze with cottages and trees on a cream ground with scratched mottoes (Fig. 140). These cottages are painted in pigment colours in a 'soft focus' style with rather more artistic feeling than the sharply outlined cottages of the Watcombe Pottery.

It is believed that the Dorset Pottery also did a version of the 'Scandy' pattern, but examples of this are less common (and probably earlier) than the cottages. Other decorative patterns included both stylized and naturalistic representations of flowers, done directly on to the brown body instead of the cream ground used for the cottage wares.

Most of these brown-bodied wares are incised with pattern numbers which are unusual in that they incorporate the size of the article in inches. The pattern numbers of articles decorated with cottages always end with the letter R (possibly for 'Rustic'); but the factory mark: the word 'Dorset' incised or impressed, or an impressed crown with the words 'CROWN DORSET', is only occasionally present.

The Crown Dorset Pottery was at its most productive in the mid-'twenties. Although badly damaged by fire in 1925 it was rebuilt and continued in business until 1937, when it finally closed.

7.5. THE WESTON-SUPER-MARE POTTERY

Articles of terracotta and glazed red earthenware are occasionally encountered which, although they strongly resemble certain types of Torquay pottery, do not bear a Torquay mark. Some of these will be found on close inspection to have a circular, but usually only partly decipherable, mark that includes the place name 'Weston-super-Mare'. The Weston-super-Mare Pottery in North Somerset is mentioned in Llewellynn Jewitt's *Ceramic Art of Great Britain* (1883) as the 'Royal Pottery', and at that time was run by a Mr Matthews. Prior to 1870 the owner had been a Mr Phillips. Although the firm specialized in garden pots, and acquired the prefix 'Royal' because it supplied large numbers of ordinary flower-pots to the royal household, it was specially praised by Jewitt for its hand-modelled 'baskets of flowers' in terracotta. These were of great delicacy and, as mentioned in Section 2.1, must have been similar to those made at Watcombe during its early years.

Various small vases from the Weston Pottery, some thrown and other probably slip-cast, have been seen decorated with simple sprays of flowers done in oil paint, and probably date to the 1890s. The mark at this time was simply 'WESTON-SUPER-MARE' arranged in a circle, but it is so small that it appears to the naked eye to be no more than the accidental impression of a small toothed wheel. However, the colour of the terracotta is much more like one of the early Torquay potteries than any of the later imitators, being a pale creamy red.

In the present century the Weston Pottery was operated by the firm of T.W. Lemon & Son, using the trade name 'WESUMA' to describe its wares. It is possible, therefore, that the Mr Lemon who, with Mr Crute, founded the Daison Pottery in Torquay was a member of this family of potters.

During the 1920s some attractive glazed articles were made, with painted decoration on a vivid blue ground, that strongly resemble the wares then being produced by the Daison and Barton potteries in Torquay. The small spill vase shown in Fig. 141, for example, is decorated with an interesting version of the 'Kingfisher' pattern, while the other vase illustrated is decorated in the same manner with a named cottage. The usual mark of this period was of the same form as the earlier one but slightly larger, and incorporated the name of the firm, with the words 'WESUMA POTTERY' in the centre, rubber-stamped in black under the glaze.

7.6. THE PLYMOUTH COXSIDE POTTERY

At the time of writing, the only evidence of the production of Torquay-type slip-wares in Plymouth is a teapot and stand, the former impressed on its base with the words 'PLYMOUTH/ GAS-FIRED'. The shape of this teapot is similar to the 1476 Aller Vale/Watcombe pattern and the decoration, a good version of the 'Scandy' design, is competently done on a light orange body similar to that of many articles of Watcombe manufacture in the early 1920s.

Little is known about the Pottery that produced such wares, but it is assumed to have been a firm working on or near the site of the Plymouth Pottery Company in the Coxside district of Plymouth mentioned by Jewitt and others as having been established in the 1850s. The fact that this business was adjacent to the local gas works supports the likelihood that the kilns were fired by gas — always an unusual feature of a British pottery.

It may be concluded that if the Coxside Pottery imitated one type of Torquay ware it no doubt made others, and the discovery of further examples is awaited with interest.

MARKS OF OTHER POTTERIES

EXETER ART POTTERY

60.

EXETER
ART
POTTERY
ENGLAND

Impressed mark, 1892—1896.
Sometimes with pattern
number adjacent.

61 (a)

EXETER ART POTTERY ENGLAND

62

Impressed marks incorporating
pattern number, 1892—1896.
Mugs usually have the pattern
numbers 60 to 62.

(b)

MADE AT THE EXETER ART POTTERY ENGLAND

60

o

HART & MOIST, EXETER

Most, but not all, twentieth century articles were clearly marked with the factory stamp. Nineteenth century wares appear to be unmarked, but may have had scratched marks which were rendered undecipherable by the glaze. No pattern numbers or craftsmen's marks have been seen.

62.

H.M. EXETER

The usual impressed mark, c.1900—c.1934. It is believed that a semi-circular rubber-stamped mark was occasionally used after the Great War, but details are not available.

THE DEVON TORS POTTERY, BOVEY TRACEY

Some articles made at this Pottery were unmarked. In particular, the large number of scent bottles produced were often unmarked or marked with the name of the retailer.

63.

**DEVON
TORS
POTTERY**

The usual impressed mark, 1920—1970? The word 'Bovey', or the letter 'B' is sometimes separately impressed.

64.

DT

Rubber-stamped underglaze mark attributed to the Devon Tors Pottery. Date uncertain.

BOVEY TRACEY ART POTTERY

It is believed that most articles made at this Pottery were given a factory mark.

65.

**BOVEY TRACEY
ART POTTERY
DEVON**

The standard black rubber-stamped mark. c.1922—c.1940.

THE CROWN DORSET POTTERY, POOLE

Many articles produced by this firm were unmarked.

66.   *Dorset*   Incised mark; probably 2nd decade of the 20th century.

67.   CROWN DORSET   Impressed mark. c.1920—1937.

68.   *42/3″R*   Type of mark incised on articles decorated with cottages. The first part is the shape number, the second number is the size in inches, and the letter indicates the style of decoration.

THE WESTON-SUPER-MARE POTTERY

69.   WESTON-SUPER-MARE POTTERY   Small impressed mark found on 19th century terracotta wares.

70.   T.W. LEMON & SON / WESUMA / POTTERY / WESTON~SUPER~MARE   Black, rubber-stamped, mark used on glazed wares, probably from c.1920.

71.   T W Lemon Son / Weston-s Mare

Incised mark on larger articles made in the 1920s and '30s.

THE PLYMOUTH (COXSIDE) POTTERY

72.      Impressed mark seen on a teapot. Possibly 2nd decade, 20th century.

APPENDIX I

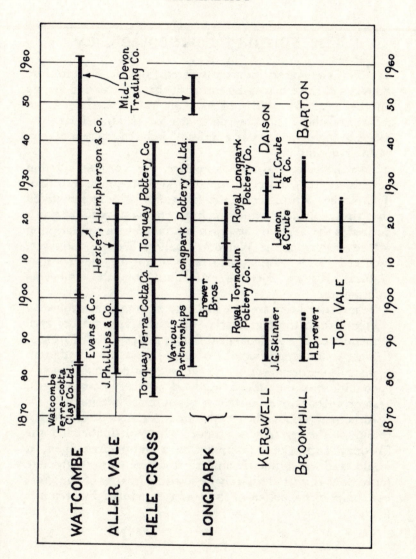

Chronological table of the old Torquay potteries.

APPENDIX II

The Torquay Terracotta Clay

The Torquay pottery industry differed from the Staffordshire Potteries of the nineteenth century in that it depended mainly on the local availability of its basic raw material — red terracotta clay. This clay never existed in large beds, and seems to have occurred as a series of isolated pockets of very variable quality.

Like the pottery Works themselves, the Torquay clay has never been the subject of much serious attention. Professor T.C. Archer, writing in the *Art-Journal* in 1878, merely stated that 'the (geological) formation from which this peculiar clay is derived is the Triassic', and then continued with a description of the scenery of the Watcombe valley. We are, however, indebted to Dr Norman Harris, Curator of the Torquay Natural History Society's Museum, for the following information:

'I have not been able to find any reference in geological literature to the pottery clay deposits. They are not even mentioned in the Geological Survey's *Memoir of Torquay*, but I would think that the occurrence was not continuous since it has been ascribed to the weathering under tropical conditions of the pre-existing land surface; in other words, some authorities think that it is a form of laterite.'

Although various nineteenth-century writers described the colour of the terracottas produced by Watcombe and the Torquay Terra-Cotta Company on a comparative basis, it would need a colorimetric analysis to define them in absolute terms. But this would hardly be justified in view of the great variability of the colour of the pottery produced by even one firm.

APPENDIX III

Aller Vale Pattern Codes

The following Table lists all those Pattern Codes, as defined on p.123, which are known to have been scratched on articles made at the Aller Vale Pottery, together with a few which appear to conform to the series but have only been seen on Watcombe or Longpark articles. Some of these codes, particularly the N series, were subsequently used by other potteries.

It should be noted that many standard patterns — including the 'Old Rhodian' designs, the sailing boats, and the cottages — do not appear to have been given codes, while articles are occasionally found with the wrong code for the decoration they bear.

The absence of an entry against certain letters in the Table does not imply that they were not used, only that examples have not been encountered. Collectors may therefore enter in the blank spaces any other codes of which they may have evidence.

LETTER	NUMERAL	DESCRIPTION
A	1	Running design of flowers and leaves in red, green, blue, and yellow on white body.
	3?	Abstract pattern of coloured bands and motifs on white body.
B	1	Coloured scrolls on white ground or body.
	2	Coloured scrolls on dark green ground.
	3	Coloured scrolls on dark blue ground.
	4	Yellow and cream scrolls, with large comma-shaped motif, on dark green ground.
	5	As B.4, but white scrolls on blue ground.
C	1	Blue scrolls on white body ('Sandringham' pattern).
	2	The 'Forget-me-not' pattern (blue dots surrounding a red boss, with green leaves).
D	1	—
	2	—
	3	White scrolls on dark blue or green ground.
E	—	—
F	1	—
	2	—
	3	White daisy motif on mid-blue ground.
	4	—
	5	Loose sprays of white flowers and leaves on mid-blue ground.
G	1	Green glaze over clear, on white ground or white body ('Normandy' pattern; known as 'Green-and-Straw' at Watcombe).

LETTER	NUMERAL	DESCRIPTION
H	–	–
I	1?	The 'Scandy' pattern on a dark blue ground.
	2?	The 'Scandy' pattern on a dark green ground.
	3	–
	4	'Abbots Kerswell', or 'Daisy' pattern on amber glazed motto ware.
J	2?	Cream-coloured flowers on a dark blue ground.
K	1?	As K.2, but on a white body or ground.
	2	Flowers painted in coloured slips, usually on dark green ground.
	3	–
	4	–
	5	–
	6	Place name painted in cream slip on dark green ground.
L	–	–
M	1	All-over green translucent glaze.
	2	Edward VII coronation pattern.
N	1	'Scandy' pattern.
	2	'Coloured Cockerel' pattern.
	3	'Black Cockerel' pattern (Only seen on Watcombe and Longpark articles).
	4	Plain green ground.
	5	–
	6	Running border of green leaves and blue flowers.
	7	–
	8	–

LETTER	NUMERAL	DESCRIPTION
N	9	Running border of double and single ovals in red, green, and cream slip, with black dots ('Ladybird' pattern).
O	—	—
P	—	—
Q	1	Scratched-outline designs filled in with coloured glazes and pigments.
R	—	—
S	1	—
	2?	Modified 'Scandy', on green ground.
	3	'Neo-Rhodian' pattern on khaki ground.
	4?	Modified 'Scandy', on pink ground.
T	—	—
U	3	Scroll design with fish-head terminal in Q.1 style.
V	—	—
W	—	—
X	—	This character has been seen incised on several Aller Vale pieces, but does not appear to relate to the decoration.
Y	1	Code applied to articles half-dipped, diagonally, in white slip, with a motto scratched through the slip.
Z	1	Blue scroll design, with incised outline, on brown ground. (On white stoneware vase.)

APPENDIX IV

Inscriptions on Torquay Pottery

In this Appendix will be found a list of typical mottoes and verses chosen at random from the very large number that have been noted on articles of Torquay pottery. The only selection that has been applied has been to restrict the number of simple inscriptions of the commonest type found on cups, cream dishes, and teapots.

These mottoes have been grouped under headings according to their subject and, although in some cases it has been difficult to decide on the most appropriate classification, it will be seen that Proverbial and Sentimental statements together account for nearly one third of the total. Patriotic sentiments are much less common than might be expected for the period when this ware was produced while, surprisingly, dialect inscriptions account for only a small proportion of the total. This may be because most of the dialect is found on tea-wares, and only a few typical examples out of the enormous variety have been listed here. It should also be mentioned that all but two of the inscriptions recorded have been incised; the exceptions, of Watcombe manufacture, being slip-trailed like icing-sugar on a cake.

Analysing these inscriptions in another way — according to the potteries that did them — shows that the Longpark factory, as might be supposed, contributes more than one third of the total, followed by Aller Vale and Watcombe. But it must be remembered that many of the mottoes were used by several potteries, sometimes with slight variations. No mottoes have been seen on articles produced by the Daison or Barton potteries, and the small number of mottoes from other firms reflects their size rather than the proportion of motto ware produced. As mentioned in the text, it is believed that many of the mottoes were introduced to the potteries by customers, who were invited to write suitable lines in the visitors' books in the firms' showrooms.

Where the source of a motto is known it has been noted afterwards in italics, although the exact wording and spelling often differs from the original.

1. Conduct

No path of roses leads to glory.   Watcombe

Little duties still put off   Watcombe
Will end in never done,
Bye-and-bye is soon enough
Has ruined many a one.

Tis deeds alone must win the prize.   Longpark

Lives of great men all remind us   Watcombe
We can make our lives sublime,
And departing leave behind us,
Footprints in the sands of time.
Longfellow: A Psalm of Life

Success comes not by wishing   Brewer (Longpark)
But by hard work bravely done.

If you your lips would keep from slips,   Aller Vale
Five things observe with care:
Of whom you speak, to whom you speak,
And how, and when, and where.
W.E. Norris: Thirlby Hall

Do the work that's nearest,   Aller Vale
Though its dull at whiles;
Helping, when you meet them,
Lame dogs over stiles.
Charles Kingsley: The Invitation

The friends thou hast, and their adoption tried,   Hart & Moist
Grapple them to thy soul with hoops of steel.
Shakespeare: Hamlet

Whatever you are, be that.   Hart & Moist
Whatever you say, be true.
Straightforwardly act,
Be honest in fact,
Be nobody else but you.

The world has battle-room for all,   Longpark
Go fight and conquer if you can.
But if you rise, or if you fall,
Be each, pray God, a gentleman.

Straight is the line of duty,   Aller Vale
Curved is the line of beauty,
Follow the one and you will see,
The other ever following thee.
After William MacCall

2. Devotion

Be the day weary, or be the day long,   Longpark
At last it ringeth to evensong.
Quoted by Tankerfield

There's a Divinity that shapes our ends,   Watcombe
Rough-hew them how we will.
Shakespeare: Hamlet

Walk life's dark path, they seem to say,   Watcombe
With love's divine fore-knowing
That where man sees but withered flowers,
God sees the sweet flowers growing.
The Rev. Hugh MacMillan D.D. (late of Greenock)

God's ways seem dark! but soon or late   Aller Vale
They touch the shining hills of day.

JOHN PIPER, PORTLAND, TIPPERARY, 1889
O shepherd true and tender,   Aller Vale
O refuge proved and tried,
O strong and sure defender,
Do thou with us abide.
We stand as little children,
Before thy mercy's door,
Come down to us, O Father,
And lead us evermore.

3. Dialect, and other Languages

From Waterford. Arragh, be aisy wid ye!	Longpark

If you can't be aisy, be as aisy as you can.	Various

Dawnt'ee urry, dawnt'ee vlurry,   Longpark
Nothing gude is got by worry.

Here's tae mysel, as bad's I am.   Aller Vale
Here's tae ye a', for as gude's ye are.
For as bad's I am, an as gude's ye are
I'm as gude's ye are, for as bad's I am.
Old Scottish toast

Bon Jour!   Watcombe

Dawnt'ee be found out now!   Longpark

Môr o can yw Cymru i gyd.   Watcombe
(The whole of Wales is a sea of song)

Dawntee try tu rin bevore yu kin walk.   Longpark

Du not cross the bridge until yer cum tu it.   Torquay Pottery

Gi a little, tak a little,   Aller Vale
When there's nocht — tak a'.

4. Domestic Activities

O list to me ye ladies fair,   Watcombe
And when ye wish to curl your hair,   Longpark
For the safety of this domicile,
Pray place your lamp upon this tile.
  (On a lamp stand)

Snore and you sleep alone.   Longpark
  (On a candlestick)

Gude things be scarce,   Watcombe
Take care of me.
  (On a jug)

Pleasant Dreams.   Brewer (Longpark)
A light in the Dark.
  (On a pair of candlesticks)

The last in bed puts out the light.   Longpark

Lets to bed, said sleepy head.   Torquay Pottery
  (On a candlestick)

5. Food, Drink, and Tobacco

O for the herrings and the good brown beef,   Aller Vale
And the cider and the cream so white.
For they are the making of the jolly Devon lads
To play and eke to fight.

Drink like a fish — water only.   Brewer (Longpark)

They say that drink leads to the Devil,   Watcombe
But a thought has just entered my head:
If a man can't drink while he's living,
How in Hell can he drink when he's dead?

Tobacco — Help yersel.   Brewer (Longpark)
  (On a tobacco jar)

A match for any man.   Longpark
  (On a match-holder and striker)

When work is done, the pipe don't shun.   Watcombe

Strike me and I'll light.   Aller Vale
  (On a match-holder and striker)

A pla(i)ce for Ashes.   Longpark
  (On a fish-shaped ash-tray)

Water is good outside and in,   Aller Vale
To quench the thirst and cleanse the skin.

6. Humour

Don't worry and get wrinkles,   Watcombe
Smile and have dimples.

If you've got the pip, don't squeak.   Watcombe

Fellow feeling makes us wondrous kind,   Hart & Moist
But I wonder if the poet would change his mind
If in a crowd one day he were to find
A fellow feeling in his coat behind?
The first line is from David Garrick: Prologue

Better wait on the cook than the doctor.   Watcombe

Better be out of the world than out of the fashion.
                               Brewer (Longpark)

Be happy while you're living   Aller Vale
For you're a long time dead.

If you're down in the mouth,   Watcombe
think of Jonah,
He came up alright.

Many are called, but few get up.   Longpark

From rocks and sands and barren lands,   Aller Vale
Good fortune set me free.
And from great guns and women's tongues,
Good Lord deliver me.

7. Mealtime

Help yourself. Nobody's looking!   Aller Vale

Don't spill the tea!   Aller Vale

Demsher craim — tak en try et.   Brewer (Longpark)

You may get better cheer,   Watcombe
But none with better heart.

Be aisy with the craim.   Longpark

When you've finished pouring tea,   Longpark
Place the teapot down on me.
   (On a teapot stand)

Take a little toast.   Watcombe
   (On a very small toast rack)

Unless the kettle boiling B,   Aller Vale
Filling the teapot spoils the T.

Some hae meat that canna eat!   Aller Vale
an some would eat that want it.
But we hae meat an we can eat!
sae let the Lord be thankit.
   (Round the rim of a bowl with, at the bottom:)
There's Mair in the Kitchen.
Burns: The Selkirk Grace

8. Morality

Errors, like straw, upon the surface flow.   Torquay Pottery
Dryden: Prologue, All for Love

For every evil under the sun   Longpark
There is a remedy, or there is none.
If there be one, try and find it.
If there be none, never mind it.
Adapted from anonymous lines in a book of Maxims
published in 1843

Have courage, boys, to do the right.   Aller Vale
Be bold, be brave, be strong.
By doing right you gain the might
To overcome the wrong.

P

Earth I am, et es most tru.   Aller Vale
Despise me not, for so be you.

If each man in his measure   Aller Vale
Would do a brother's part,
To cast a ray of sunlight
Into a brother's heart,
How changed would be our Country,
How changed would be our poor,
And then might Merry England
Deserve her name once more.

9. Patriotism

See! in Victoria's Glorious Reign   Aller Vale
How England does its best attain.
Because thro' Sixty years she's been
Our Great, our Good, our Gracious
1837 — Queen — 1897
      (On a jug commemorating the Diamond Jubilee)

God bless you, Tommy Atkins,   Aller Vale
Here's your country's love to you.
South Africa 1899 — 1900
      (On articles commemorating the Boer War)

Send them victorious,   Aller Vale
Happy and glorious.
Long to reign over us,
God save them both.
      (On articles commemorating the coronation of
      King Edward VII and Queen Alexandra)

10. Precepts and Maxims

Vessels large may venture more,   Torquay Pottery
Little boats must keep the shore.

Put your shoulder to the wheel.   Brewer (Longpark)

There's a saying old and musty,   Aller Vale
   yet it is ever true.
'Tis never trouble trouble,
   till trouble troubles you.

Keep your face to the sunshine   Watcombe
and the shadows will fall behind.

Lucky people have their days,   Aller Vale
And those they choose.
Unlucky people have their hours,
And those they lose.

To all friends be one.   Brewer (Longpark)

The best physic is fresh air,   Hart & Moist
The best pills is plain fare.

Fretting amends no broken dishes,   Hart & Moist
Brings us none of all our wishes.

Would you live an angel's days?   Aller Vale
Be honest, just, and wise always.

Better to sit still than rise to fall.   Torquay Pottery

Do noble things, not dream them all day long.
        Torquay Pottery

Ride over all obstacles and win the race.   Brewer (Longpark)

We're not the only pebbles on the beach.   Longpark

Do not burden today's strength   Aller Vale
   with tomorrow's loads.

See a pin let it stay   Brewer (Broomhill)
Bad luck yours all the day.

Never quit certainty for hope.   Hart & Moist

11. Proverbial

Sow a character,   Watcombe
reap a destiny.

A good name is better than riches.   Watcombe

A good name keeps its lustre in the dark.   Watcombe

Actions speak louder than words.   Watcombe

Every Why hath a Wherefore.   Torquay

A kindness today is worth six in the future.   Longpark

Right wrongs no one.   Torquay Pottery

The early bird catches the worm.   Brewer (Longpark)

Every blade of grass has its   Hart & Moist
own drop of dew.

A rolling stone gathers no moss.   Watcombe

A bird in the hand is   Watcombe
worth two in the bush.

Hear all, see all, say nothing.   Longpark

Ill blows the wind that profits nobody.   Watcombe

To a friend's house the road is never long.   Watcombe

He who hesitates is lost.   Torquay Pottery

Lost time is never found.   Torquay Pottery

The night is long that never finds a day.   Brewer (Longpark)

12. Sentiment

Full many a shaft at random sent   Aller Vale
Finds mark the archer never meant.
A many a word at random spoken
Can wound or heal a heart that's broken.
After Scott: The Lord of the Isles

When this you see remember me.   Brewer (Broomhill)

Be a little deaf and blind,   Watcombe
Happiness you'll always find.

There's gladness in remembrance.   Watcombe

A hedge between keeps friendship green.   Longpark

If life an empty bubble be,   Watcombe
How sad for those who cannot see
A rainbow in the bubble.

May the wing of friendship never moult a feather.   Longpark

May the hinges of friendship never grow rusty.
                     Brewer (Broomhill)

Only the memory of the just   Aller Vale
Smells sweet, and blossoms in the dust.
After James Shirley, 1596—1666

Life has many shadows,   Hart & Moist
but'tis the sunshine makes them.

Gather ye roses while ye may,   Tormohun (Longpark)
Old Time is still a-flying.
After Robert Herrick, 1591—1674

Two men look through the same bars;   Torquay Pottery
One sees the mud, the other the stars.
Rev. F. Langbridge: A Cluster of Quiet Thoughts, 1896

Q

230

Kind words are the music of the world.   Watcombe

13. Work and Play

All things must yield   Aller Vale
   to Industry and Time.
None cease to rise but those
   who cease to climb.

Work while you work,   Longpark
Play while you play.
That is the way
to be cheerful and gay.

Let us then be up and doing   Aller Vale
With a heart for any fate.
Still achieving, still pursuing,
Learn to Labour and to wait.
Longfellow: A Psalm of Life

APPENDIX V

Bibliography

Books:

Jewitt, Llewellynn: *Ceramic Art of Great Britain*, 1883.
Baring-Gould, S.:   *A Book of the West*, Part I, Devon, (chap.xvi) 1899.
Blacker, J.F.:   *A.B.C. of 19th Century English Ceramic Art*, c.1910.
Phillpotts, Eden: *Brunel's Tower*, 1915.
Hughes, G. Bernard: *Victorian Pottery and Porcelain*, 1959.
Wakefield, Hugh: *Victorian Pottery*, 1962.
Lloyd Thomas, E.:   *Victorian Art Pottery*, 1974.

Papers and Articles:

Phillips, John: *Transactions of the Devonshire Association*: 1881, p. 214, 'The Potter's Art in Devonshire'. 1889, p. 159, 'A Cottage Art School in a Devonshire Village'. 1890, p. 255, 'Arts and Crafts in Devon'.

Art-Journal, The: *The Watcombe Terra-Cotta Works*, Vol. XI, p. 200, (1872). *The Torquay Terra-Cotta Company Limited*, Vol. XVI, p. 215, (1877). Prof. T.C. Archer, *The Watcombe Terra-Cotta Company*, Vol. XVII, p. 172, (1878). H. Snowden Ward, *Two Devonshire Potteries*, 1900, p. 119.

Monkhouse, Cosmo: *The Potteries of Aller Vale*, The Magazine of Art, 1891, p. 349.
Country Life: *Aller Vale Pottery*, March 9th, 1901.

Reade, Brian: *Fine Examples of Victorian Potters' Skill*, The Times, Aug. 14th, 1965.

Insh, J. Rodger: *'From Mother Earth I Took my Birth'*, (Devon motto ware), Art & Antiques Weekly, Vol. 17 No.2, Nov. 23rd, 1974.

Index

Fig.1. Early Watcombe terracotta vase decorated with applied motifs, turquoise enamel, and gilding. Height: 380 mm (15.0 in). Marks: Nos. 2 (printed) and 16(b). c. 1875.

Page 246
Fig.2. Early Watcombe terracotta vase, of classical form, decorated with moulded swags on a central light-coloured ground. (The base is a replacement.) Height: 405 mm (16.0 in). c. 1875.

Fig.3. Watcombe terracotta vase, of two-part construction, decorated with a transfer-printed and pigment-coloured frieze of classical figures (the cover is missing). Height: 380 mm (15.0 in). Marks: Nos. 1 & 16(a) with '1844' painted. c. 1875.

Fig.4 (above). Group of early Watcombe terracotta articles, including: footed bowl with mottle-glaze interior, vase and miniature bowl decorated with white vitreous beads, vase with carved decoration enamelled in four colours, and tray with moulded rim. Marks: Nos. 2, 3, 5, & 16(d).

Fig.5. Watcombe terracotta copy of the Portland Vase. This type of ware was sometimes described as 'Watcombe Wedgwood'. Unmarked. Mid-1870s.

Copyright, Exeter Museums

Page 248

Fig.6. Watcombe terracotta bust of John Bright, the Corn Law reformer, after an original by A. Bentley. Unmarked, except for sculptor's name and turner's stamp No. 16(b) (on the base). The retail price in the 1870s was 18/-.

Fig.7 (below). Watcombe architectural roundel with cherub's head in relief. Unmarked. Early 1870s.

Copyright, Exeter Museums

Page 249

Fig.8. Watcombe figure group, believed to be 'Cupid and Psyche', in three shades of terracotta. Height: 490 mm (19.3 in). Marks Nos. 2 & 4, with 'PATENT' also printed. c. 1875.

Fig.9 (left). Watcombe terracotta figure, decorated with blue, yellow, and black enamels. (A copy of 'WINTER' from the Bristol/Derby china set of the Seasons). Height: 254 mm (10.0 in). Mark: No. 2 impressed. c. 1880.

Fig.10 (below). Watcombe terracotta figure of an angel, with the parian porcelain version by Byng & Grondahl (Copenhagen) from which it appears to have been directly moulded. Note the reduction in size due to shrinkage. Height: 203 mm (8.0 in). Marks: No. 2 printed, with '1888' painted. Late 1870s.

Page 251

Fig.11. Watcombe terracotta vase in French style, decorated with parrots in coloured enamels and subsidiary gilding. Height: 430 mm (17.0 in). Mark: No. 5 printed, with '5621' painted. Early 1880s.

Fig.12 (above). A photograph of the Watcombe Pottery at the end of the nineteenth century. (Reproduced from the *Art-Journal*, with acknowledgements to Virtue & Company Ltd.)

Fig.13 (below). Large terracotta panel (now painted) on the wall of a house formerly known as 'Etruscan Lodge' and the home of Mr Charles Brock, the first Manager and Art Director of the Watcombe Terra-Cotta Co.

Fig.14. Watcombe terracotta figure /plant holder, in the form of a paper-boy, entitled 'BRISK'. This can be dated from the placard to c. 1880. Height: 230 mm (9.0 in).

Fig.15. Watcombe terracotta figure entitled 'THE WHISTLING COON'. Height: 430 mm (17.0 in). Mark: No. 17(f). c. 1890.

Fig.16 (left). Engraving of the figure group by G. Focardi, known as 'YOU DIRTY BOY' and made by the Watcombe Pottery as an advertisement for Pears soap from about 1880 until 1914. (Reproduced with acknowledgements to A. & F. Pears Ltd.)

Fig.17 (below). Watcombe plaque decorated in oils with kingfishers, probably at the Pottery. This subject was popular both at Watcombe and Hele Cross and developed into the 'Kingfisher' pattern of the 1920s. (See also Figs. 122, 136 and Plate VI.) Diameter: 254 mm (10.0 in). Unsigned, but impressed Mark No. 4. Late 1880s.

Fig.18 (above). Two Watcombe pilgrim flasks decorated in oils, probably at the Pottery. The larger, painted on the reverse with marguerites and a bee, is 205 mm (8.2 in) tall and carries marks No. 2 and 16(h), with '1184' impressed. c. 1885.

Fig.19 (right). Large Watcombe plaque, finely painted in oils with orchids and signed on the face by Holland Birbeck. Mark: No. 2. c. 1890.

Fig.20 (left). Early classical-type Watcombe vase, impasto decorated in the mid-'eighties with fashionable 'aesthetic' flowers on a stippled ground and glazed all over, the neck and base painted to resemble marble. Height: 343 mm (13.5 in). Marks: Nos. 6 (printed, with 'PATENT'), 16(g), and '985' impressed.

Fig.21 (below). Group of Watcombe vases of the 1890s, ornately decorated underglaze with flowers and birds. (Reproduced from the *Art-Journal*, with acknowledgements to Virtue & Company Ltd.)

Page 257

Fig.22 (above). Examples of Watcombe 'Egyptian Ware', introduced in 1900, but now seldom seen. (Reproduced from the *Art · Journal*, with acknowledgements to Virtue & Company Ltd.)

Fig.23 (right). Watcombe hanging jardiniere, made of white clay and finished in flown red and green glazes. c. 1895. Diameter: 254 mm (10.0 in). Marks: Nos. 2 & 16(h), with '389' impressed.

Page 258

Fig.24 (above). Watcombe ornament in the form of a girl holding a net. Moulded from white clay and finished with coloured glazes. c. 1895. Height: 152 mm (6.0 in). Mark: No. 2.

Fig.25 (right). Watcombe white terracotta plate with elaborate relief-moulded design picked out in oil colours. c. 1890. Diameter: 240 mm (9.5 in). Marks: No. 2, with '5212' & 'C' impressed.

Fig.26. Watcombe slip-decorated ware of Aller Vale type, c. 1905. The vase finished with 'Scandy' and a scratched motto; the jug with trailed slip on a green ground. Height of vase: 254 mm (10.0 in). Marks: vase No. 8 (without 'England') & '1963 N.1' incised; jug, No. 7 with '154' incised.

Fig.27 (below). Examples of Watcombe 'Motto' or 'Cottage' Ware. Each article bears a scratched motto or place name on the opposite side. Note that Watcombe cottages nearly always have two storeys. Marks: Nos. 7, 11, 13, & 14. Period covered c. 1917—c. 1950.

Fig.28. Watcombe vase decorated with fish in coloured slips under a thick clear glaze. Height: 203 mm (8.0 in). Mark: No. 7. c. 1910.

Fig.29. Example of 'Watcombe Porcelain', decorated with transfer-printed and hand-coloured floral design on the turned and glazed dark red body. Note the moulded handle. Height: 152 mm (6.0 in). Marks: Nos. 10 & 16(d). c. 1880.

Page 261

Fig.30. Watcombe faience biscuit barrel, decorated with fishing boat. c. 1915. Height: 125 mm (4.9 in). Mark: No. 11 with 'Made in England'.

Fig.31. Watcombe faience articles decorated with flowers, 1915—20. Left to right: spill vase with blue clematis on a black trellis, plate with pink rose on a streaky mauve ground, jug with pink and green clematis. Note typical black rims. Marks: (l. to r.) No. 9, No. 8, No. 7. Height of jug 203 mm (8.0 in).

Fig.32 (above). Watcombe faience dish and jug decorated with named topographic subjects: 'Cockington Church' and 'Woodhall Spa, Tower on the Moor', done in characteristic dark green and gingery brown, with sprayed green borders. c. 1915. Marks: No. 7; the dish also has No. 17(d) incised.

Fig.33 (right). Watcombe vase decorated underglaze with outline of a canary, done by painting in black over a yellow ground. Height: 238 mm (9.4 in). Mark: No. 8 (without 'England') and '1507' incised. c. 1910.

Fig.34 (above). Examples of Watcombe 'Art Green Ware', 1915—1920. The jugs are finished in green glaze over white slip, and the bowl in green glaze direct on the brown body. The body of the jug on the right is left as rough terracotta. Height of taller jug: 254 mm (10.0 in). Marks: (l. to r.) 'Watcombe/885' incised; No. 7, with 'England' and '1571' incised; No. 12.

Fig.35 (below). Watcombe tile, or plaque, with sgraffito inscription and slip-painted border in the old Aller Vale 'Forget-me-Not' pattern of green leaves and blue flowers. Dimensions: 203 mm x 133 mm (8.0 in x 5.5 in). Marks: No. 7, with 'C.2' incised. c. 1910.

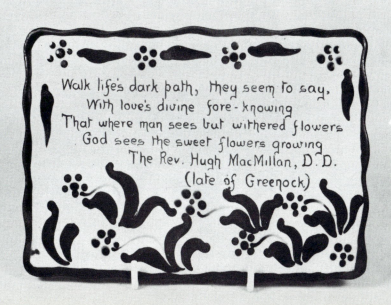

Fig.36 (above). Examples of Watcombe pottery decorated with the
'Kingfisher' pattern on a blue ground.
(Watcombe kingfishers usually dive
from left to right; except on articles
made as pairs, where the birds dive in
opposite directions for symmetry.)
Height of vase: 203 mm (8.0 in).
Marks: (l. to r.) Nos. 12, 8, & 14.
1925—1930.

Fig.37 (below). Watcombe   articles
with blue-ground decoration, late
1920s. The bowls have a multi-coloured
'jazz' pattern, and the *pot-pourri* jar a
geometric design. The teapot is decorated with a coloured low-relief moulding
of the 'Widecombe Fair' characters.
Marks: all No. 14, teapot also has
'1476' incised.

Page 265

Fig.38 (above). Three Watcombe articles made about 1930. Left: vase with painted and sprayed design and eggshell glaze. Centre: jug with splashed colours under an eggshell glaze. Right: small pot decorated with white heather on a mauve ground. Height of jug: 138 mm (5.4 in). Marks: all No. 14.

Fig.39 (below). Some Watcombe employees of the mid-1920s. Standing: left to right: Fred Clements (chief handler), Eddy Clements (handler), unknown, — Hicks (turner), Fred Dart (thrower). Kneeling: Charlie Annan (turner), Ernie Clements (wedger).

Page 266

Fig.40 (above). Three Watcombe slip-decorated jugs made about 1950. These are decorated with (from l. to r.): Cockington Forge, the 'Polka Dot' pattern (in this example, blue dots on a yellow ground), and the traditional 'Cottage' pattern. Height of largest jug: 110 mm (4.3 in). Marks: all No. 15.

Fig.41 (below). One of the last vases made at the Watcombe Pottery; finished in black, with a sgraffito design, over a white body. Height: 152 mm (6.0 in). c. 1960.

Page 267

Fig.42 (above). 'Tap set' by the Torquay Terra-Cotta Co. The vessels are undecorated, but glazed inside. Height of jug: 204 mm (8.0 in). Mark: No. 18 impressed under jug and tray, No. 24(b) on beakers. Late 1870s.

Fig.43 (below). Terracotta figure of a girl by the Torquay Terra-Cotta Co., entitled 'HOMELESS', after an original by Emmeline Halse. Length: approx. 380 mm (15.0 in). Marks: No. 21 (printed) and 'Emmeline Halse fecit' (moulded). c. 1885.

Page 268

Fig.44 (above). Terracotta figure of a young sculptor by the Torquay Terra-Cotta Co., inscribed: 'Zocchi Sc./ REGISTERED/August 24th. 1877'. Height: 456 mm (18.0 in). Mark: No. 18.

Fig.45 (right). One of a pair of terra-cotta figures by the Torquay Terra-Cotta Co. Probably based on 'The Bather' by J.M. Mohr. Height: 370 mm (14.5 in). Mark: No. 18. c. 1882.

Fig.46 (left). Small terracotta bust of the Prince of Wales (later Edward VII) attributed to the Torquay Terra-Cotta Co. Note the detail. Height: 100 mm (4.0 in).

Fig.47 (below). Terracotta vase, with finely turned body decorated with black and white enamels, by the Torquay Terra-Cotta Co. Late 1870s. Height: 266 mm (10.5 in). Mark: No. 21 (printed).

Fig.48. Terracotta vase by the Torquay Terra-Cotta Co. The frieze
of classical figures, in puce pigment on an off-white ground, is
attributed to Alexander Fisher snr. Subsidiary decoration is puce
enamel with gold and black lines. Late 1870s. Height: 185 mm (11.2
in). Marks: Nos. 18 & 16(b).

Fig.49 (left). Jug, attributed to the Torquay Terra-Cotta Co., and decorated with a swallow and bulrushes in coloured enamels. Height: 228 mm (9.0 in). c. 1885.

Fig.50 (below). Plaque by the Torquay Terra-Cotta Co. decorated in the Pottery with a view of Kenilworth castle done in fired black pigment with white enamel highlights. Diameter: 280 mm (11.0 in). Marks: No. 21, with 'W' painted in black. c. 1885.

Fig.51. One of a pair of vases, decorated underglaze on a yellow ground over a red body. The birds are in brilliant colours and the leaves outlined in gold. Attributed to Holland Birbeck at the Torquay Terra-Cotta Co. Unmarked. Height: 380 mm (15.0 in). c. 1895.

Fig.52 (left). Glazed vase, attributed to the Torquay Terra-Cotta Co. and believed to be an example of 'Crown Devon Ware'. The apple blossom decoration in pink and white is on a dark green ground, with the base and neck left as glazed terracotta. Height: 200 mm (7.9 in). c. 1895.

Fig.53 (right). Large turned vase decorated with speckled flown glazes in green and grey over a red body. An example of the Torquay Terra-Cotta Co.'s 'Stapleton Ware', early 1890s. Height: 305 mm (12.0 in). Mark: No. 19 impressed, with No. 24(c).

Page 274

Fig.54. Early terracotta plaque, decorated in oils, by the Torquay Pottery, c. 1910. Diameter: 240 mm (9.4 in). Mark: No. 25.

Fig.55. Group of Torquay Pottery articles decorated underglaze with sailing boats in pigment colours, c. 1920. Height of jug: 144 mm (5.7 in). Marks: Jug, No. 28 (?); vases, No. 32.

Page 275

Fig.56. Photograph of the proprietor and employees of the Torquay Pottery,
c. 1915. Note examples of decorated ware in foreground.
Left to right,
Back row: Reg. Brimicombe (thrower), Reg. Head (mould maker and handler),
Jim — (clay digger), A. Heywood (dipper), F. Nicholls (decorator), unknown,
L. Southwood (wedger).
Middle row: Vincent Kane (modeller), J. Black (kiln placer), Harry Crute
(decorator), C. Radmore (decorator), Gerry — (ball boy), S. Holland
(saggar-maker), H. Shrodzinski (gloss dipper).
Front row: G. Coker (handler), Harry Birbeck (decorator), Charlie Wonnacott
(thrower), Enoch Staddon (proprietor), J. Way (foreman), H. Brown (turner),
B. Birbeck (decorator).

Page 276

Fig.57 (above). Torquay Pottery tea-service, decorated underglaze with red cabbage roses on a cream ground, with sprayed green borders. Mark: No. 29(b). c. 1915.

Fig.58 (below). Dressing-table set by the Torquay Pottery, decorated in pigment colours with pink roses and green leaves on a streaky dark pink ground over white. The central article is a hatpin holder. Unmarked. c. 1920.

Fig.59 (left). Vase by the Torquay Pottery decorated with a peacock, in low relief and simply coloured, on a cream ground shading into black. Height: 305 mm (12.0 in). Mark: No.30. c. 1917.

Fig. 60 (below). Torquay Pottery jardiniere decorated with a version of the 'Kingfisher' pattern on a yellow ground. Height: 182 mm (7.3 in). Mark: No. 31. c. 1922.

Fig.61 (above). Torquay Pottery: candlestick decorated with moulded and applied butterfly, and candle snuffer with moulded peacock. c. 1912. Mark: No. 25.

Fig.62 (below). Electric table lamp base in the form of an owl, by the Torquay Pottery, early 1920s. Height: 380 mm (15.0 in). Unmarked.

Fig.63 (above). Slip dipping and handling at the Torquay Pottery, early 1920s. Note the small Toby jugs.

Fig.64 (below). Quart face jug, slip cast and painted underglaze as one of the characters of the 'Widecombe Fair' ballad. From a set of eight modelled by Vincent Kane at the Torquay Pottery. (Very few of these were made.) c. 1920.

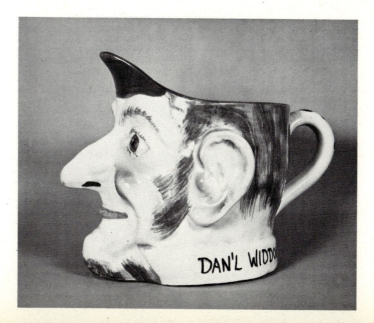

Page 280

Fig.65 (above). Two Torquay Pottery articles decorated with applied low-relief mouldings and finished in underglaze pigment colours. (a), (left): mug with the characters of 'Widecombe Fair'; (b), (right): jug with view of Clovelly. Early 1920s. Heights: mug, approx. 100 mm (4.0 in); jug, 130 mm (5.0 in). Marks: mug, No. 31; jug, No. 27.

Fig.66 (below). Small vase by the Torquay Pottery, decorated with a cottage in pigment colours over a blue ground, and with 'F. Bowden/Jan 17 1923' painted in black on the base. Height: 114 mm (4.5 in).

Fig.67 (above). Group of articles made by the Torquay Pottery in the early 1920s, decorated with applied low-relief mouldings of birds and finished in colours over a blue ground. The 'sponged' foliage is typical. (Compare with Fig.59.) Height of tall vase: 265 mm (11.3 in). Marks: Nos. 28, 31, & 32.

Fig.68 (below). Centre: vase by the Royal Torquay Pottery, decorated with green and orange 'leaves' on a mottled blue ground; left: small pot with similar decoration by the Bovey Tracey Art Pottery. Right: pot decorated with butterfly on plain blue ground by the Torquay Pottery. Height of vase: 203 mm (8.0 in). Marks: 32 & 73.

Fig.69 Covered vase of Oriental shape by the Royal Torquay Pottery.
Decorated as early faience with blue pigment on a white ground. Mid-1920s.
Height: 305 mm (12.0 in). Mark: No. 32.

Fig.70 (left). Royal Torquay jug of characteristic shape decorated with a band of coloured motifs on a white ground, above a blue body. Late 1920s. Height: approx. 200 mm (7.8 in). Marks: No. 32 with '515 No. 24 Dec.' painted (presumably a pattern code).

Fig.71 (below). Group of small slip-decorated bottles, intended to contain 'Devon Violets' and other scents. These were made by most of the Torquay potteries in the present century, and are usually unmarked.

Fig.72. Terracotta bottle vase, with corrugated foot in darker clay. One of the first products of the rebuilt Aller Art Pottery in the early 1880s. Height: approx. 200 mm (8.0 in). Mark: No. 34(b).
Copyright, Exeter Museums

Fig.73. Moulded terracotta jug, with low-relief decoration in pre-Columbian style, made at the Aller Art Pottery in the early 1880s. Height: approx. 150 mm (6.0 in). Mark: No.34(a).
Copyright, Exeter Museums

Page 285

Fig.74. Throwing at the Aller Vale Pottery. Note the string-driven wheels and massive construction of the building. (Reproduced from the *Art-Journal*, with acknowledgements to Virtue & Company Ltd.)

Fig.75. Decorating Aller Vale pottery in the late 1890s. (Reproduced from the *Art-Journal*, with acknowledgements to Virtue & Company Ltd.)

Fig.76 (above). Early glazed Art-ware jug attributed to the Aller Pottery. Slip-decorated, on a blue-grey ground, over a dark red body, with 'daisies' and 'tadpoles' in yellow and terracotta slip. The side bears a scratched motto. Height: approx. 100 mm (4.0 in). Mark: No. 35. c. 1885.

Fig.77 (below). Three styles of Aller Vale decoration, all on a red body. Left to right: 'Huacco Marble' (streaky coloured glazes), the 'Ladybird' pattern (N.9), and 'Black Lacquer' (black glaze with flowers in oil paint). See text for dates.

Fig.78 (right). Aller Vale vessel in the form of a bird; slip-decorated, on a white ground over a dark red body, in the style known as 'Old Rhodian'. This pattern may have been the basis of the later 'Scandy' design (Fig. 93). Height: 152 mm (6.0 in). Mark: No. 36, very rubbed. c. 1887.

Fig.79(a) (above). Early Aller Vale jug decorated underglaze on a blue-grey ground with pixies dancing, done in sgraffito and coloured slips. Height: 114 mm (4.5 in). c. 1887.

(b) (below). Recessed (turned) base, showing Mark No. 36.

Fig.80 (above). Aller Vale tea service made from white clay and decorated underglaze with scrolls in coloured slips. Mark: No. 38(b). Late 1880s.

Fig.81 (below). Three examples of Aller Vale 'Sandringham Ware', c. 1890. This pattern consisted of scrolls done underglaze in blue slip, usually on a white body, but the depth of colour and sharpness of outline is very variable. Height of jug: 147 mm (5.8 in). Marks: Nos. 37 & 38(b), with 'C.1' incised.

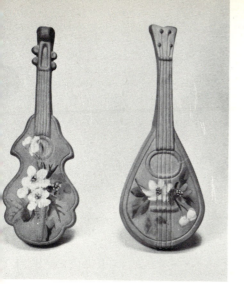

Fig.82 (left). Two small terracotta ornaments, in the form of musical instruments, decorated in oils. Left: violin by the Watcombe Pottery. Right: mandolin by the Aller Vale Pottery. Height: approx. 165 mm (6.5 in). Marks: Nos. 3 & 38(b). Both c. 1890.

Fig.83 (below). Aller Vale stoneware jug with impressed decoration produced by means of 'runners'. An example of the Pottery's range of domestic wares in buff-coloured clay. Height: 180 mm (7.0 in). Mark: No. 37. Probably late 1880s.

Fig.84 (left). Small Aller Vale stoneware vase with buff-coloured body, decorated with an incised scroll design and finished in blue and brown under a clear glaze. Height: 106 mm (4.2 in). Mark: No. 37 with '1253 Z.1' incised. Late 1890s.

Fig.85 (below). Group of Aller Vale articles decorated underglaze with scroll patterns in multi-coloured slips, mainly on dark green or blue grounds over a red body. The bowl has a white body. Period: 1890—1900. Marks: Nos. 38 (a) & (b), and 39. Pattern codes B.1, B.2, & B.4.

Page 291

Fig.86 (above). Large Aller Vale vase decorated underglaze with stylized flowers and foliage done in coloured slips on a light green ground over a red body. Height: 200 mm (7.9 in). Marks: No. 122, with '1072' incised. c. 1897.

Fig.87 (below). Three jugs, of a type originated by Aller Vale, with handles passing through pierced rims. Left to right: Brewer (Longpark), Watcombe, Aller Vale. Period: 1900–1905. The Aller jug is 150 mm (5.8 in) high and has mark No. 39 impressed, with '648 Q.1' incised.

Page 292

Fig.88. Aller Vale jug in red earthenware body, of waisted form with pinched rim. Decorated underglaze with flowers done in coloured slips on a dark green ground. Height: 207 mm (8.2 in). Mark: No. 38(a), with '885 K.2' incised. c. 1895.

Fig.89. Aller Vale mug made to commemorate the Boer War. The figure of the soldier is an applied moulding and the inscription reads: 'God Bless you Tommy Atkins, here's your Country's love to you. South Africa 1899—1900'. Height: 127 mm (5.0 in). Mark: No. 38(b).

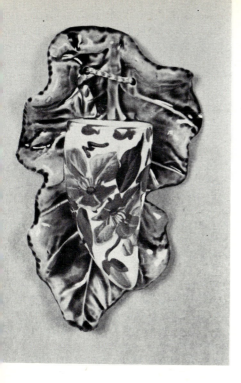

Fig.90 (left).Aller Vale wall pocket made of white clay. The backplate is pressed in the form of a leaf and glazed green. The horn-shaped pocket is decorated under a clear glaze with a clematis flower. Height: 215 mm (8.5 in). Mark: No. 38(a). Late 1890s.

Fig.91 (below). Pair of moulded Aller Vale grotesque cats, finished in green glaze with glass eyes. That on the left is made of white clay, the other of red/brown clay. Height of taller: 230 mm (9.0 in). Marks: No. 38(b), one with 'DEVON' and the other with 'ENGLAND'. c. 1900.

Page 294

Fig.92. Aller Vale grotesque face jug. The features are coloured in red and ochre on a dark blue body and the handle at rear is moulded as a pigtail. Height: 152 mm (6.0 in). Mark: No. 38(b). Late 1890s.

Fig.93 (below). Group of articles decorated in coloured slips under a clear glaze, with the 'Scandy' pattern (N.1). The jug on the left and the cup on the right are Aller Vale and bear mark No. 38(b). The plate and sugar bowl are Watcombe, with Mark No. 7. Period: 1890—1905.

Fig.94 (above). Aller Vale plate and jug decorated in the 'Abbots Kerswell' (I.4) style with mottoes, 'daisy', and 'tadpole' motifs under an amber glaze. Marks: No. 38(b) with 'ENGLAND' and pattern codes.

Fig.95 (below). Aller Vale bowl decorated underglaze with the 'Coloured Cockerel' pattern and a motto. Diameter: 152 mm (6.0 in). Marks: No. 38(b) ?, with '975 N.2' incised.

Page 296

Fig.96. Group of articles decorated with flown green glaze in the style known at Aller Vale as 'Normandy' (G.1) and at Watcombe as 'Green-and-Straw'. Centre: Aller vase with white ground over a red body. Right: Watcombe jug with white body. Left: vase, probably Brewer (Longpark), with red body. All 1900—1905 period.

Fig.97. Aller Vale pitcher made of light red clay and decorated on a white ground with sgraffito designs filled with coloured glazes. This type of decoration, usually marked with the 'Q.1' code, was popular c. 1900. Another example is shown in Fig.87.

Fig.98. Aller Vale vase with pinched fan-shaped neck, decorated with a dolphin. Probably intended to display dried grasses or feathers. Height: 115 mm (4.5 in). Mark: No. 39. Early 1900s.

Fig.99. Aller Vale vase of the Edwardian period decorated on a white ground with a green and terracotta floral design between dark green borders. Height: 152 mm (6.0 in). Mark: No. 40, with 'England'.

Fig.100(a) (above). Three terracotta plaques made at the Longpark Terra-Cotta Works, decorated in oils. That on the right is initialled 'S.S.' in black (see also Fig.108). Diameter of largest: 344 mm (13.4 in). All c. 1890.

(b) (below left). Impressed mark (No. 41) on the plaques shown at (a). The blank sector is believed to have originally contained the word 'CHINA'.

Fig.101 (right). Two-handled Longpark mug with fine light red body, slip-decorated with the 'Coloured Cockerel' pattern. Note the typical Longpark border. Height: 153 mm (6.0 in). Mark: '26 N.2' heavily incised. Brewer period, c. 1900.

Fig.102 (above). Longpark jug of the Brewer period decorated in slip and sgraffito with the 'Black Cockerel' pattern. Height: 132 mm (5.4 in). Mark: possibly No. 42. c. 1900.

Fig.103 (right). Vase in light red clay decorated in cream and brown slips over a sage green ground. Attributed to the Brewer brothers at Longpark, c. 1900. Height: 140 mm (5.5 in). Mark: No. 42 (?).

Page 300

Fig.104 (above). Longpark articles of the Brewer and Bulley periods, slip-decorated with sailing boats. Period: c. 1900—c. 1913. Those with fore-and-aft sails are the earliest. Marks: 42 & 44(a).

Fig.105 (below). Longpark tea-service of the Brewer period, slip-decorated on a dark brown body with a cottage design (note the timber-framed construction of the buildings). c. 1904. Mark: No. 42.

Fig.106 (above). Group of slip-decorated articles typical of the Longpark Pottery during the Bulley period (1905–1913), decorated with scrolls, 'Scandy', and the 'Black Cockerel'. Marks: Nos. 43 & 44(a).

Fig.107 (below). Two Longpark inscribed plaques, and a plate, of the Bulley period (c. 1910). The article on the left was intended as a stand for a curling iron lamp, and the same verse was used at Watcombe. Marks: Nos. 42 & 43.

Page 302

Fig.108. Tall Longpark jug, slip-decorated with a continuous
scene of ruined buildings by a stream, against an evening sky
(possibly based on the painting of Tintern Abbey by B.W.
Leader). This has the initials 'S.S.' incised after the pattern
number (189) and may have been done by a member of the
Skinner family. Height: 254 mm (10.0 in). Factory mark: No.
43. c. 1910.

Fig.109. Group of small pieces of 'Tormohun Ware'. Apart from their marks these are typical products of the Longpark Pottery just before the Great War. The two small articles in front are an ink bottle and a pepper-pot. Marks: No. 47(a) impressed or printed.

Fig.110 (below, left). Large Tormohun jug, decorated as faience in pigment colours on a cold white ground. Height: 190 mm (7.5 in). Marks: Nos. 43 & 46. c. 1912.

Fig.111 (below, right). Small Tormohun vase decorated with a hand-coloured view of Cockington village and finished with sprayed green borders. The outlines and title are transfer printed. Mark: No. 47(b). c. 1913.

Fig.112 (left). Humorous Tormohun figure of a pig, slip-cast in white clay and glazed pale green. Height: 153 mm (6.0 in). Mark: No. 47(a). c. 1912.

Fig.113 (below). Four-necked vase by the 'Royal Longpark' Pottery, decorated with a swagged design in coloured slips and blue glaze. Height: 110 mm (4.3 in). Mark: No. 48. c. 1916.

Page 305

Fig.114. Royal Longpark candlestick decorated with a moulded and
sgraffito dragon and finished in
coloured slips and glazes. Height:
190 mm (7.5 in). Mark: No. 48. c.
1918.

Fig.115. Royal Longpark bowl decorated with applied roses and leaves and
finished in mottled cream and green slips. Diameter: 230 mm (9.0 in). Mark:
No. 48. c. 1922.

Page 306

Fig.116. Royal Longpark two-handled mug in white clay. Decorated in Barnstaple style with a frog and water-weed, done in coloured slips and flown blue and green glazes. This is marked with the same pattern (shape) number as the Brewer mug of Fig. 101. Height: 153 mm (6.0 in). Mark: No. 48 with '26' incised. c. 1916.

Fig.117 (below). Longpark ash-tray in the form of a fish, with appropriate punning motto. This is mentioned in Eden Phillpotts' novel *Brunel's Tower*. Length: 145 mm (5.7 in). Mark: No. 50. c. 1920.

Fig.118. Longpark vases decorated in slip with daffodils on a green ground. Mark: No. 44(a). c. 1915.

Fig.119. Three Longpark vases decorated underglaze with pigment colours. Left to right: pink roses and black stems on streaky mauve ground over white; red roses on white ground with green borders; dark blue iris on light blue ground. Marks: (l. to r.) Nos. 50, 45, 44(b). Period: 1915—1925.

Fig.120 (above). Group of Longpark articles decorated underglaze with coloured butterflies on a streaky mauve ground. Marks: Nos. 44(a) & (c). c. 1922. (Compare with Fig. 126).

Fig.122(a) (above). Group of Longpark articles of the 1920s decorated with the 'Kingfisher' pattern on a blue ground. (Longpark kingfishers, except on the left-hand articles of pairs, always dive from right to left; compare with Fig. 36). Marks: Nos. 44(a) & 50.

(b) (below right). Unusual mark on base of the 'Kingfisher' vase of Plate VI, giving the names of three Longpark 'managing directors'.

←

Fig.121 (opposite page). Long-park articles decorated with cockerels: all of the 'black', or 'N.3', variety, except for the small candlestick on the left, which is marked as 'coloured' ('N.2'). Marks: Nos. 43 & 44(a). Period: 1905—1920.

Page 310

Fig.123 (above). The buildings once occupied by the Longpark Pottery (*Brunel's Tower*) as they are today (mid-1970s). The kilns, now demolished, were to the right of the picture, while the small extension in the foreground served as the manager's office.

Fig.124 (right). Terracotta bust of Joseph Chamberlain 'Published by the Kerswell Art Pottery Co.' and modelled by the proprietor, Mr W.J. Skinner, in 1887. Height: 230 mm (9.0 in). Mark: No. 52.

Fig.125 (left). Small vase, slip-decorated with coloured scrolls on a dark green ground, by the Brewer Pottery at Broomhill. A motto inscribed on a cream band over a scroll background is typical of this firm. Height: 94 mm (3.7 in). Mark: No. 53. c. 1890.

Fig.126 (below). Group of early Lemon & Crute (Daison) wares, decorated underglaze with butterflies and white heather, done in pigment colours on a streaky mauve-pink ground. Mark: No. 54. c. 1922.

Fig.127 (above). Group of small articles made at the Daison Pottery. Those in the lower row are painted with Harry Crute's sea-gulls on a pale blue ground. The bowl and jug above are decorated in a raised slip design over a scumbled orange ground. Marks: Nos. 54 (painted), & 57. c. 1925.

Fig.129 (above). Group of small articles made at the Barton Pottery in the 1920s. The jugs have a bright blue ground, that on the right being slip-decorated with a sea-gull. The jam jar (centre) is splashed with thin pigment colours on a white ground. Marks: all No. 58.

Fig.128 (opposite page). Pair of Daison vases decorated underglaze in pigment colours, probably by Harry Crute, with blue-tits on a light blue ground. Note the Barnstaple-type handles. Height: 195 mm (7.7 in). Mark: No. 55. c. 1927.

Fig.130 (right). Large Daison vase decorated in subdued colours and signed by Harry Birbeck. Height: approx. 254 mm (10.0 in). Mark: No. 56. Probably late 1920s.

Page 314

Fig.131. Large Barton vase decorated underglaze on a blue ground with a moonlight scene of a cottage amongst trees. Height: 305 mm (12.0 in). Mark: No. 58. c. 1927.

Page 315

Fig.132(a). Exeter Art Pottery mug inscribed with a quotation from 'The Merchant of Venice' and finished in an amber glaze over a white ground. Height: 127 mm (5.0 in). Mark: No. 61(a). c. 1895.

Fig.132(b). Exeter Art Pottery mug decorated under a clear glaze with white slip over a blue-grey ground. The opposite side bears a motto and the spurious date '1815'. Height: 122 mm (4.8 in). Mark: No. 60. c. 1895.

Fig.133. Three articles attributed to the Hart & Moist Pottery, c. 1900. The mug on the left is slip-decorated in 'rosemaling' style under an amber glaze, with a motto on the reverse. The tankard (centre), with a long motto on a blue-grey ground, is of a type also made at Aller. Note the typical 'wings' motif. Height of tankard: 195 mm (7.7 in).

Fig.134. Large, moulded, Hart &
Moist jug with raised decoration,
coloured cream and yellow, on a
dark green ground. Although this
is 177 mm (7.0 in) wide, it is only
83 mm (3.2 in) from front to back.
Mark: No. 62. c. 1905.

Fig.135 (below). Group of early twentieth-century Hart & Moist articles,
slip-decorated in imitation of Aller Vale pottery of the 1890s. The ground
colours are cream or green; except for the pot at the top left, which has white
scrolls on blue. Note the typical pointed centre of this firm's 'Scandy' design.
Marks: all No. 62.

Page 317

Fig.136. Bovey Art Pottery
bowl, decorated with a version of the 'Kingfisher'
pattern on a cream ground.
Incised underneath: '"Gertie"
Summerfield, Bovey Tracey
19-10-22'.

Fig.137. Bovey Art Pottery
vase finished, in imitation of
ancient Egyptian ware, with
thin black glaze on the body
and stripes of bright colours
on the neck. Note the turned
spiral groove simulating a
coiled construction. Height:
215 mm (8.2 in). Mark: No.
65. c. 1924.

Fig.138. Group of articles made at the Devon Tors Pottery. Left to right: small beaker with sgraffito representation of 'Bill Brewer'; bowl and cover with cottage design; small jug decorated in the same style as the vase of Fig. 137. Marks: beaker and jug, No. 63; bowl, No. 64. Period: second quarter, twentieth century.

Fig.139. Three small kilns of *the* Bovey Pottery. These are now the only surviving kilns of all the old South Devon factories.

Page 319

Fig.140. Small vase and candlestick by the Dorset Pottery decorated with cottages and trees, in a 'soft focus' style, in imitation of Torquay ware. Each has a motto on the other side. Height of vase: 73 mm (3.0 in). Marks: vase, '43/3R'; candlestick, ?/10R. c.1920.

Fig.141. Three articles made at the Weston-super-Mare Pottery. Left: late nineteenth century terracotta vase decorated in oils with flowers; centre and right, two vases of the 1920s, decorated in pigment colours on a bright blue ground with a cottage and a version of the 'Kingfisher' pattern. Height of taller vase: 152 mm (6.0 in). Marks: Nos. 69 & 70.